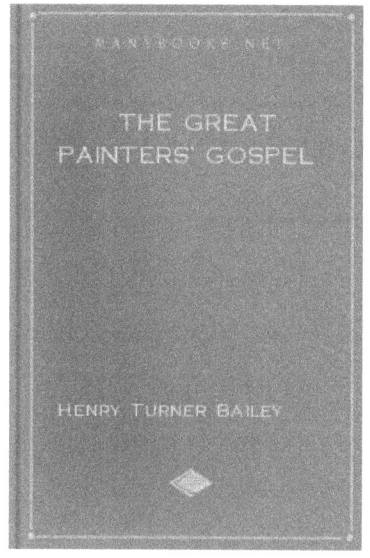

Great Painters' Gospel, by Henry Turner Bailey

Title: The Great Painters' Gospel Pictures Representing Scenes and Incidents in the Life of Our Lord Jesus Christ

Author: Henry Turner Bailey

Release Date: January 5, 2012 [EBook #38500]

Language: English

Character set encoding: ISO-8859-1

*** START OF THIS PROJECT GUTENBERG EBOOK THE GREAT PAINTERS' GOSPEL ***

Produced by Michael Gray, Diocese of San Jose

[Illustration: "I am the Light of the World"] Holman Hunt. 1827- *"I am the Light of the World."*

THE GREAT PAINTERS' GOSPEL

PICTURES representing scenes and incidents in the life of Our Lord Jesus Christ

With scriptural quotations, references and suggestions for comparative study

By HENRY TURNER BAILEY

W A WILDE COMPANY BOSTON MASS USA

TABLE OF CONTENTS.

"His name is John" Luke 1:63 FRA ANGELICO

Childhood.

Nativity.

"No room for them in the inn" Luke 2:7 MERSON "The angel of the Lord came upon them" Luke 2:9 PLÖCKHORST "Glory to God in the highest" Luke 2:14 HOFMANN "Found Mary and Joseph and the babe" Luke 2:16 LEROLLE "Wondered at those things" Luke 2:18 CORREGGIO BOUGUEREAU MÜLLER

Presentation.

"Now lettest thou thy servant depart Luke 2:29 FATTORINO in peace" "This child is set for the falling Luke 2:34 CHAMPAIGNE and rising up of many in Israel" "A sword shall pierce thine own soul" Luke 2:35 BORGOGNONE Anna coming up at that instant Luke 2:38 BOURDON BARTOLOMMEO

Adoration of Magi.

The star stood over the child Matt. 2:9 HOFMANN They came to the house Matt. 2:11 MALDINI And they worshipped the child Matt. 2:11 LUINI And gave unto him gifts Matt. 2:11 BONIFAZIO

Flight into Egypt.

An angel appeared to Joseph in a dream Matt. 2:13 CRESPI He arose and departed Matt. 2:14 FÜRST With the child and his mother Matt. 2:14 PLOCKHÖRST Guided by the angel HOFMANN Into Egypt Matt. 2:14 BENZ In Egypt MERSON Was there till the death of Herod Matt. 2:15 MORRIS

Return to Nazareth.

Mother and child MURILLO "Grace of God was upon him" Luke 2:40 MURILLO Daily life at Nazareth HOFMANN

Youth.

Visit to Jerusalem.

"They went up to Jerusalem" Luke 2:42 MENGELBERG In the midst of the doctors Luke 2:46 HOFMANN LAFON "When they saw him they were amazed" Luke 2:48 DOBSON "Son, why hast thou thus dealt with Luke 2:48 HUNT us?"

Silent Years at Home.

The carpenter's son HUNT "Breaking home ties" PLOCKHÖRST [The youthful John] Luke 1:80 DEL SARTO [The forerunner] Matt. 3:1-4 TITIAN

Manhood.

Temptation.

"Worship the Lord thy God" Matt. 4:10 SCHEFFER "Left him and behold angels came" Matt. 4:11 HOFMANN

Beginning of Public Service.

"Behold the Lamb of God" John 1:29 BIDA "Jesus as he walked" John 1:36 GRÜNEWALD A marriage in Cana John 2:1 VERONESE

Early Judean Ministry.

Cleansing the temple KIRCHBUCK "He drove them all out" John 2:15 HOFMANN Visit of Nicodemus John 3:1-21 UNKNOWN

Return through Samaria.

"Thou wouldst have asked of him" John 4:10 BILIVERTI "Worship the Father in spirit and John 4:23 DORÉ truth" "God is a Spirit" John 4:24 HOFMANN

Call of the Four.

"I will make you fishers of men" Matt. 4:19 ZIMMERMAN "Depart from me for I am a sinful man" Luke 5:8 RAPHAEL

Early Galilean Ministry.

"He healed all that were sick" Matt. 8:16 SCHÖNHERR HOFMANN MAX Calling of Matthew Matt. 9:9 CHIMENTI "Sitting at the receipt of custom" Matt. 9:9 PORDENONE "Follow me" Matt. 9:9 BIDA

At Jerusalem Again.

"Jesus saith unto him, 'Rise'" John 5:8 BIDA "He took up his bed and walked" John 5:9 VAN LINT "Afterward, Jesus findeth him" John 5:14 VAN DYCK Discussion in cornfield Matt. 12:1-8 DORÉ

Sermon on the Mount.

Christ preaching DORÉ Giving beatitudes Matt. 5:1-12 HOFMANN "Consider the lilies of the field" Matt. 6:28 LE JEUNE Prayer in secret Matt. 6:6 BIDA

Second Tour of Galilee.

The Centurion's servant Matt. 8:5-13 VERONESE Raising the widow's son Luke 7:11-17 HOFMANN Jesus in the house of Simon VERONESE "Kissed his feet" Luke 7:38 RUBENS "Thy sins are forgiven" Luke 7:48 HOFMANN "He entered into a boat" Mark 4:1 HOFMANN Parable of the sower Mark 4:3-9 ROBERT Stilling of the tempest Mark 4:35-41 DORÉ Raising of Jairus' daughter RICHTER "Taking the child by the hand" Mark 5:41 HOFMANN "Straightway she rose up" Mark 5:42 KELLER

Death of John the Baptist.

"The damsel gave it to her mother" Mark 6:28 RENI

Feeding of the Five Thousand

Blessing the food John 6:11 MURILLO

Jesus Walking on the Water

"Lord, save me" Matt. 14:30 SCHWARTZ "Wherefore didst thou doubt?" Matt. 14:31 PLOCKHÖRST

Trip into Phoenicia.

Canaanitish woman Matt. 15:21-28 VECCIO

Peter's Confession.

"I will give the keys of the kingdom Matt. 16:19 RENI of heaven" RAPHAEL

Transfiguration.

Transfiguration Matt. 17:1-8 RAPHAEL Demoniac Boy Matt. 17:14-20 RAPHAEL "He called to him a little child" Matt. 18:2 BALLHEIM

At the Feast of Tabernacles.

"Let him that is without sin cast John 8:7 HOFMANN the first stone" Jesus left alone with the woman John 8:19 SIGNOL "I am the light of the world" John 8:12 HUNT "I stand at the door and knock" Rev. 3:20 OVERBECK "I will give you rest" Matt. 11:28 PLOCKHÖRST

Perean Ministry.

The good Samaritan Luke 10:30-34 SIEMENROTH DORÉ Jesus in the home of Lazarus Luke 10:40 HOFMANN ALLORI Healing of the man born blind John 9:1-40 THEOTOCOPULI The good Shepherd John 10:1-21 PLOCKHÖRST Finding the lost sheep Luke 15:2 SCHÖNHERR MOLITOR Lost piece of money Luke 15:8 MILLAIS The prodigal son Luke 15:11-32 DUBUFE "Fell on his neck and kissed him" Luke 15:20 MOLITOR DORÉ Rich man and Lazarus Luke 16:19-31 DORÉ Raising of Lazarus John 11:1-46 BONIFAZIO PIOMBO RUBENS Pharisee and Publican Luke 18:9-14 DORÉ Christ blessing little children Mark 10:13-16 HOFMANN PLOCKHÖRST VOGEL Christ and the Young Ruler Matt. 9:16-22 HOFMANN Ambition of James and

John Matt. 20:20-28 BONIFAZIO

Passion Week.

Triumphal entry Luke 19:29-44 DEGER Christ weeps over Jerusalem Luke 19:41 EASTLAKE Tribute money DORÉ "Whose image and superscription Mark 20:24 TITIAN hath it?"

"Render to Caesar the things that Matt. 22:21 VAN DYCK are Caesar's" The widow's two mites Mark 12:41-44 DORÉ Parable of the virgins Matt. 25:1-13 POLOTY Conspiracy between Judas and Luke 22:3-6 BIDA Chief Priests The Last Supper VINCI "When he had washed their feet" John 13:12 BROWN "This is my body" Luke 22:19 BIDA "And he took a cup and gave thanks" Matt. 26:27 HOFMANN "Thy will be done" Matt. 26:42 HOFMANN "An angel from heaven Luke 22:43 DOLCI strengthening him" Kiss of Judas Matt. 26:49 SCHEFFER "Bound him and led him to Annas" John 18:12 HOFMANN Peter's denial before the John 18:17 WEST maid-servant Denial before soldiers Mark 14:54 HARRACH Trial before Pilate Luke 23:1-7 MUNKACSY "Hail, King of the Jews!" Matt. 27:29 RENI "Behold the man" John 19:5 HOFMANN CISERI Pilate's wife's dream Matt. 27:19 DORÉ

The Crucifixion.

"They led him away" Luke 23:26 HOFMANN "Weep not for me" Luke 23:28 THIERSCH "The people stood beholding" Luke 23:35 MUNKACSY The group near the cross John 19:25 MUNKASCY "Behold thy mother" John 19:27 HOFMANN Descent from the cross Mark 15:46 RUBENS Golgotha GEROME The deserted cross MORRIS

The Burial.

"They took the body of Jesus" John 19:40 CISERI "Laid him in a tomb" Mark 15:46 HOFMANN John with Mary DYCE DOBSON

The Resurrection.

"Mary was without weeping" John 20:11 HOFMANN "Tell me where thou hast laid him" John 20:15 DI CREDI "Touch me not" John 20:17 PLOCKHÖRST "Returning from the tomb" Luke 24:9 SCHEFFER

After the Resurrection.

"Jesus drew near and went with them" Luke 24:15 PLOCKHÖRST "Abide with us" Luke 24:29 HOFMANN "And he went to abide with them" Luke 24:29 FÜRST "He took the bread and blessed it" Luke 24:30 MULLER "And break and gave to them" Luke 24:30 DIETHE "And their eyes were opened" Luke 24:31 REMBRANDT "Reach hither thy hand" John 20:27 GUERCINO The Ascension Luke 24:51 HOFMANN REMBRANDT

SUGGESTIONS.

[Illustration: Capernaum] *Site of Capernaum, Sea of Galilee.*

THE USE OF PICTURES IN TEACHING.

PICTURES may hold a primary or secondary place in teaching, according to their nature and the aim of the teacher.

The text itself may be the supreme thing, and pictures become mere pictorial comments upon the text. Pictures when so used have the nature of *views* or *illustrations*. The picture at the head of this page is a view. It is reproduced from a photograph taken directly from nature. Such pictures are of great value in building up in the mind clear images of objects or of scenes beyond the pupil's reach. A map means almost nothing to a person unfamiliar with the country, unless by means of numberless views the appearance of the country has been made known to the mind. Every teacher in Sunday-school should have a collection of photographic views of the historical sites of the Bible, of implements, household utensils, articles of dress, etc., which may be used to make clear the Biblical references to such things. Without such illustrations words may convey little or no meaning.

The first picture upon the next page may be called an illustration. To a person unfamiliar with the text it might convey any meaning but the true one; but to one familiar with the story of Christ and the rich young ruler it is wonderfully graphic and satisfactory. The words of the text take on a deeper meaning as they are studied in the light of this picture. Because Hofmann is an artist, a man gifted with imagination, he sees more clearly, more vividly than the average person. Seen through his eyes what was before vague and unconvincing becomes definite and powerful. Before seeing the picture the pupil had heard the words:"Jesus, looking upon him, loved him." Now with the picture he *sees* that Jesus loves him and is anxious to have him decide for life everlasting. Before "the poor" were abstract; now they become a concrete reality. Before the pupil had been told that the young man had "great possessions;" now he sees that he had also health and beauty and intelligence, greater possessions than land and gold. The Sunday-school teacher is fortunate who has at his command pictures which illustrate, which make luminous the text. Plates 11, 20, 34, 39, 47, 62, 70, 101, 106, 133, and 143 may be mentioned as notable examples of good illustrations to supplement the text.

[Illustration: Christ and the Young Ruler.] Plate 112. *Christ and the Young Ruler.* H. Hofmann. 1824-

The picture itself may be the object of study, and the text become a commentary upon the picture. For example, consider this picture by Holman Hunt. Every detail has something important to say to the pupil. The postures of these people and the costumes say "oriental." The profuse ornamentation both of the architecture and the various furnishings speak of extraordinary conditions. This is the temple which was the wonder of the age (see Mark 13:1), and these are the people who loved to go about in long clothing, and who "devoured widows' houses" to be rich. (Matt. 23:14.) This boy with his pure face and far-away-gazing eyes is he who had thoughts about "his Father's house." The look in the woman's face is appreciated in the light of what she is recorded as having said, "I have sought thee sorrowing." (Luke 2:48.) That she rather than her husband should speak to him is no surprise to one familiar with Matt. 1:18-25. The faces of these serious-looking men must be read in the light of the words, "And all that heard him were amazed at his understanding and answers." One man has an ornamental box in his hand. What is that for? Another has a similar box upon his forehead. Why? Deut. 6:6-8 and Matt. 23:5 will help answer those questions. A man is begging at the entrance. It is not extraordinary in the light of Acts 3:1, 2, and Mark 14:7. He begs in vain outside, while within a servant brings wine to refresh those who will not so much as lift a finger to help the burdened. (Matt. 23:4.) Beyond the beggar craftsmen are still at work upon the temple. Yes, because when this child Jesus first visited the temple it was not completed. "Forty and six years was this temple in building." (John 2:20.) Birds are flying in and out! "Yea, the sparrow hath found a house, and the swallow a nest for herself, . . . even thine altars, O Lord of Hosts." (Ps. 84:3.) The little boy with the fly-driver tells the season of the year, the light and the few worshippers and the idle musicians tell the time of day. Everything has a message, even the ornament upon wall and floor! That tells whence the Jews derived their art. This picture is more than a commonplace illustration of a single text: it is a graphic presentation of an era. The particular event is shown in its historical setting. The picture is a supreme work of art.

[Illustration: Finding of Christ in the Temple.] Plate 35. *Finding of Christ in the Temple.* Holman Hunt. 1827-

If pictures of this sort are to be studied, every pupil in the class should have a copy. The teacher's business is to direct the pupil to individual observation and inquiry. The perpetual questions should be, What do you see? What does it mean? Why is that here? What does it contribute to the total content of the picture? What does the picture as a whole have to say? Plates 8, 9, 18, 25, 29, 33, 40, 81, 89, 93, 110, 139, 153, 159, and 167, might be mentioned among those especially worthy of this analytical and exhaustive study.

Occasionally pupils will find both interest and profit in the comparative study of a series of pictures. For example take the five plates of The Annunciation, pages 9 and 10. After the facts have been determined by a study of the text, the investigation may proceed as follows: What are the essential elements found in all the pictures alike? Which artist has told the story most simply and directly? The different artists have emphasized or given special attention to some one phase or phrase. Which has embodied more perfectly the first, or the second, or the third? Which has introduced elements of his own? Why? Do they help? Which has, on the whole, told the story most vividly? Which most beautifully? A study of this group of pictures in the light of such notes as will be found printed therewith, will enable any teacher to formulate for himself a plan for studying any other group of pictures.

In such study it is essential that each pupil be supplied with a complete set of the pictures to be compared.

[Illustration: Madonna of the Shop.] *Madonna.* Dagnan-Bouveret.

But the picture itself is sometimes not a thing to be consciously analyzed and inventoried; it is simply a thing of beauty, "its own excuse for being;" it is something to be received as a whole with thankfulness, like the odor of wild grape vines, or the form of a calla lily, or the color of a sunrise, or the music of wind in pine trees. Such a picture is this Madonna of the Shop, by Dagnan-Bouveret. One may think for a moment now and then of how well the picture is composed, of how perfect a master of his art the man must be who can make spots of paint suggest wood and metal, linen and wool, soft flesh and softer light, but the mind returns again and again to the contemplation of the wondrous sweet face of the Virgin, whose deep eyes see unspeakable things. One comes to love such a picture as a dear familiar friend, and to yield to its gentle influence as to moonlight upon the sea. The contemplation of such pictures is one of the purest pleasures of life, a foretaste of the sight of "the King in his Beauty."

THE GREAT PAINTERS' GOSPEL.

THE GREAT PAINTERS' GOSPEL.

[Illustration: The Annunciation.] *The Annunciation.* Titian.

THE ANNUNCIATION.

The angel Gabriel was sent from God to a virgin whose name was Mary. The angel said "Hail, Mary, highly favored, blessed art thou among women." (Luke 1:26-28.) Mary is supposed to have been in a house of worship at the time (like Hannah, 1 Sam. 1:9-18, and Zacharias, Luke 1:8-13), hence the beautiful surroundings; and to have been at prayer, as suggested by the kneeling posture and the book.

The dove is a symbol of the Holy Ghost (Luke 3:22). The beam of light symbolizes the going forth of divine power (Hos. 6:5). The angel is borne upon a cloud (Ps. 104:3), and carries a rod or scepter, symbols of authority (Ex. 4:1-5, Esther 4:11). The lily is introduced as a symbol of perfection and purity (Song 2:2; compare also Num. 17:8). Titian has depicted the instant when the angel says "Hail, Mary." He has introduced emblems of the ideal woman (Prov. 31:13, 14, 26, etc.).

[Transcriber's Note: As you may note, each plate is introduced with the artist's name and the plate number. In the original source, this text was bolded, not italicized.]

Hofmann, Plate 1, shows the moment when Gabriel says: "Blessed art thou among women." (Luke 1:28.) In this picture only, the angel approaches from behind. The picture recalls the experience of another Mary (John 20:14).

Guido Reni, Plate 2,, has chosen the instant when Gabriel says, "Thou hast found favor with God." The infant angels represent, perhaps, "the spirits of love, intelligence and innocence," [1] and accompany the Divine Presence because of the words of Christ, when speaking of children, "Their angels do always behold the face of my Father which is in heaven." (Matt. 18:10.)

Müller, Plate 3, seems to have shown the moment when Mary said, "Let it be unto me according to thy word." (Luke 1:38.) His figures and faces express less animation than any of the others.

Dosso, Plate 4, represents Gabriel as saying, "The Holy Ghost shall come upon thee and the power of the Highest shall overshadow thee" (Luke 1:35), for both the dove, symbol of the Holy Ghost, and the Highest himself, upon a cloud and accompanied with cherubs, are present. (Compare 2 Sam. 22:10-12.)

Baroccio, Plate 5, seems to have seized upon the moment when Mary has just asked "How shall this be?" (Luke 1:34). The angel is encouraging her faith by reference to Elisabeth. (Luke 1:36.)

[1] Mrs. Jameson, "Sacred and Legendary Art," vi., p. 57.

[Illustration: Annunciation to Mary.] Plate 1. *Annunciation to Mary*. H. Hofmann. 1824-

[Illustration: Annunciation to Mary.] Plate 2. *Annunciation to Mary*. Guido Reni 1575-1642.

[Illustration: Annunciation to Mary.] Plate 3. *Annunciation to Mary*. Franz Müller.

[Illustration: Annunciation to Mary.] Plate 4. *Annunciation to Mary*. Dossi Dosso. 1479-1542.

[Illustration: Annunciation to Mary.] Plate 5. *Annunciation to Mary*. F. Baroccio. 1528-1612.

THE SALUTATION.

"And in those days Mary arose and went into the hill country to a city of Judah, and entered into the house of Zacharias and saluted Elisabeth . . . and Elisabeth, filled with the Holy Ghost, said, Blessed art thou among women." (Luke 1:39-45.)

Albertinelli, Plate 6, has depicted the two women at the moment of meeting.

[Illustration: Mary's Visit to Elisabeth.] Plate 6. *Mary's Visit to Elisabeth*. Albertinelli. 1474-1515.

BIRTH OF JOHN THE BAPTIST.

Zacharias had been dumb since the moment when he doubted the prophecy of the angel. (Luke 1:20.) When the promised son was born the neighbors and friends of the mother, Elisabeth, objected to the name John. (Luke 1:57-61.)

Fra Angelico, Plate 7, has represented the moment when they appeal to the dumb father, and he writes upon a tablet the words "His name is John." (Luke 1:63.) The child, eight days old, is present to be named preparatory to circumcision. (Gen. 17:12.)

[Illustration: Birth of John.] Plate 7. *Birth of John.* Fra Angelico. 1370-1450.

THE NATIVITY.

Merson, Plate 8, has illustrated Luke 2:4-7. "And Joseph went up from Galilee into Judea unto the city of David, Bethlehem, to be enrolled, with Mary his espoused wife. And there was no room for them in the inn." Darkness covered the earth and gross darkness the people who refused lodging to such as Mary, but that night the glory of the Lord was revealed. (Is. 60:2.)

[Illustration: Joseph and Mary, Arrival at Bethlehem.] Plate 8. *Joseph and Mary, Arrival at Bethlehem.* Olivier L. Merson.

Plockhörst, Plate 14, illustrates Luke 2:8-11. And in the same country were shepherds keeping watch over their flock by night. And the angel of the Lord came and said unto them, "Fear not, I bring you good tidings of great joy. Unto you is born this day in the city of David a Savior which is Christ the Lord." The angel bears a palm branch, symbol of triumph. (John 12:13.)

[Illustration: The Angel and the Shepherds.] Plate 14. *The Angel and the Shepherds.* B. Plockhörst, 1825-

Hofmann, Plate 13, shows a company of the heavenly host praising God and saying, "Glory to God in the highest, and on earth peace, good will toward men." (Luke 2:14.) They are the first to visit the manger!

[Illustration: Bethlehem.] Plate 13. *Bethlehem.* H. Hofmann. 1824-

Lerolle, Plate 11, shows the shepherds who "came with haste and found Mary and Joseph and the babe lying in a manger." (Luke 2:15-16.) The shepherds saw, evidently from some little distance; for we have no record of their speaking to Mary or Joseph, only to others outside, after the visit. (Luke 2:17-18.)

[Illustration: The Arrival of the Shepherds.] Plate 11. *The Arrival of the Shepherds.* H. Lerolle.

Correggio, Plate 9, has expressed that surprise and wonder of the shepherds which they imparted to others when they told their story, "for all that heard it wondered at those things which were told them by the shepherds." (Luke 2:18.)

[Illustration: Holy Night.] Plate 9. *Holy Night.* Correggio. 1494-1534.

Bouguereau, Plate 10, adds to the story a dramatic touch. There are ominous shadows in the background. Mary seems troubled by the presence of the lamb, symbol of sacrifice. The angel had said "He shall save his people from their sins." (Matt. 1:21.) Does Mary seem already to behold the Lamb of God which taketh away the sin of the world? (John 1:29.) One lamb is already slain, and lies in the foreground. The shepherd with the lamb in his arms may unconsciously illustrate the Christ (Is. 40:11), and the odd disk above the head of the older shepherd, catching the light from the child, may be prophetic of saintly glory.

[Illustration: The Nativity.] Plate 10. *The Nativity.* (William) Adolphe Bouguereau. 1825-

Müller, Plate 12, gives us perhaps the prettiest, most sweetly human group of all. Some of the shepherds have arrived, others are coming; one with a lamb in his arms, another with his dogs, who seem to sympathize with their master's joyous haste. The rose of the hills, and the violet of the meadows are there as symbols of the rose of Sharon and the lily of the valley (Cant. 2:1); "The ox knoweth his owner and the ass his master's crib," and in this case the humble representatives of Israel know also, and the people consider. (Is. 1:3.)

[Illustration: The Nativity.] Plate 12. *The Nativity.* Carl Müller. 1839-

THE PRESENTATION.

His name was called Jesus, as the angel had commanded, and after forty days they brought him to Jerusalem to present him to the Lord, and to offer a sacrifice, according to the ancient law. And Simeon, waiting for the consolation of Israel, came by the spirit into the temple when the parents brought in the child Jesus; and he took him up into his arms and blessed God and said, "Lord, now lettest thou thy servant depart in peace, for mine eyes have seen thy salvation." (Luke 2:25-35.) And Anna, a prophetess of great age, coming up at that very hour, gave thanks to God and spake of him to all them that were looking for the redemption of Jerusalem. (Luke 2:36-38.)

Bartolommeo, Plate 18, depicts the moment when Simeon says "Now lettest thou thy servant depart in peace"--the *Nunc Dimittis* of the Latin Church (Luke 2:29). Joseph has the two doves for the offering (Lev. 12:6 and 8). In the distance the priest may be seen at the altar, his robe ornamented with the sacred fringe (Ex. 39:26) that there may be no mistaking him. Anna is present, and is, evidently, about to speak. The steps are of marble and the columns richly carved, because of the words of the artist-disciple recorded in Mark 13:1.

[Illustration: Presentation at the Temple.] Plate 18. *Presentation at the Temple.* Bartolommeo Del Fattorino. 1475-1517.

Champaigne, Plate 15, has chosen the moment when Simeon says to Mary, "This child is set for the falling and rising up of many in Israel." (Luke 2:34.)

[Illustration: Presentation at the Temple.] Plate 15. *Presentation at the Temple.* Champaigne. 1602-1674.

Borgognone, Plate 16, selects for his picture the last moment, when Simeon returns the child to the mother with the words "Yea, and a sword shall pierce through thine own soul, also." (Luke 2:35.)

[Illustration: Presentation at the Temple.] Plate 16. *Presentation at the Temple.* Borgognone. 1445-1523.

Bourdon, Plate 17, represents the instant when Anna arrives (at the extreme left), "coming up at that very hour." (Luke 2:38.)

[Illustration: Presentation at the Temple.] Plate 17. *Presentation at the Temple.* Sebastien Bourdon. 1616-1671.

Bartolommeo, again, *Plate 19,* adds what he pleases to the original story.

[Illustration: Presentation at the Temple.] Plate 19. *Presentation at the Temple.* Fra Bartolommeo. 1469-1517.

THE ADORATION OF THE MAGI.

Now when Jesus was born there came wise men from the east, guided by a star, which went before them till it stood over the place where the young child was. . . . And when they were come into the house they saw Jesus and Mary his mother, and fell down and worshipped him; and when they had opened their treasures they presented unto him gifts; gold, frankincense and myrrh. (Matt. 2:9-11.)

Hofmann, Plate 20, represents the arrival. The star stands above the head of the child. The tradition is that one wise man came from Europe, one from Asia and one from Africa (See *Ben-Hur*, Book I.); hence Hofmann has represented one with the oriental turban, one with a helmet having hanging side pieces like an Egyptian head dress, and one with the simple band, the white hair and flowing beard of the Druid.

[Illustration: Worship of the Magi.] Plate 20. *Worship of the Magi.* H. Hofmann. 1824-

Luini, Plate 21, following the same tradition, gives the African a dark complexion.

[Illustration: Adoration of the Magi.] Plate 21. *Adoration of the Magi.* Luini. 1460-1530.

Maldini, Plate 23, also makes one of the Magi very dark, and adds an earring as a barbaric touch. Moreover he gives each a crown (as does Luini) because the Magi were supposed to have been Kings, in fulfilment of Is. 60:3.

[Illustration: Adoration of the Kings.] Plate 23. *Adoration of the Kings.* Battista Maldini. 1537-1590.

Bonifazio, Plate 22, like Luini and Maldini, represents a large company of servants to show the importance of the Magi, and perhaps because of Is. 60:4-6.

[Illustration: Adoration of the Magi.] Plate 22. *Adoration of the Magi.* Bonifazio Veronese. 1494-1563.

THE FLIGHT INTO EGYPT.

Crespi, Plate 24, has pictured Joseph's dream. An angel of the Lord appeared to Joseph in a dream, saying, Arise and take the young child and his mother, and flee into Egypt, for Herod will seek the young child to destroy him. (Matt. 2:13.)

[Illustration: Joseph's Dream.] Plate 24. *Joseph's Dream.* Daniele Crespi.

Fürst, Plate 26, illustrates the words "And he arose and took the young child and his mother, and departed." (Matt. 2:14.)

[Illustration: Flight into Egypt.] Plate 26. *Flight into Egypt.* M. Fürst.

Plockhörst, Plate 27, shows the holy family passing through southern Judea, accompanied by cherubs, but unconscious of their presence.

[Illustration: Flight into Egypt.] Plate 27. *Flight into Egypt.* B. Plockhörst. 1825-

Hofmann, Plate 25, shows them passing through the Wilderness of Shur, Joseph with his broad axe for protection, unconscious of the guardian angel who accompanied them, to keep them in all their ways. (Ps. 91:11.) "That old serpent" is already in the wilderness, waiting! His time has not yet come.

[Illustration: Flight into Egypt.] Plate 25. *Flight into Egypt.* H. Hofmann. 1824-

Benz, Plate 28, has taken as his subject the first moment of rest in a place "even as the garden of the Lord, like the land of Egypt as thou comest into Zoar." (Gen. 13:10.) Joseph has a typical Egyptian water-jar upon his arm. The little child is pleased with the flowers, after his long journey through the desert, and holds a bunch of them in his hand. The place of rest seems to be just at the edge of the desert,--a secluded, well-watered spot, out of Herod's reach.

[Illustration: Repose in Egypt.] Plate 28. *Repose in Egypt.* S. Benz.

Merson, Plate 29, is a poetic seer as well as an artist. The sphinx riddle was "What is man?" Merson has placed the answer before the sphinx at last. He who was himself the answer to the world-old question, propounded a new question which all must answer, "What think ye of Christ" (Matt. 22:42).

[Illustration: Repose in Egypt.] Plate 29. *Repose in Egypt.* Olivier L. Merson.

Morris, Plate 30, gives us a glimpse of the life of the Holy Family during the sojourn in Egypt. Joseph is resting in the tent after his day's work, and Mary is teaching the child to walk. All are unconscious of the ominous shadow so evident now to us. The hatred which threatened the child, would not spare the man. The exile in Egypt is but the prophetic shadow of the coming event--crucifixion. The child's hands extend towards the cactus and the palm, symbols of suffering and of victory.

[Illustration: Shadow of the Cross.] Plate 30. *Shadow of the Cross.* P. R. Morris.

THE RETURN TO NAZARETH.

When Herod was dead, Joseph, instructed by an angel, brought Mary and Jesus into the land of Israel, and made them a home in Nazareth. The mother with her divine child in this Nazareth home has ever been the favorite subject with painters. "Madonna" pictures have been multiplied into the thousands. The most famous are those which were painted by Raphael,--the Sistine Madonna, Madonna of the Chair,

Madonna da Tempi, Madonna of the Goldfinch, etc.,--reproductions of which are familiar to everybody. Among other famous painters of the Madonna is *Murillo,* who, in *Plate 32,* represents the mother and child as the neighbors might have seen them in their humble home. The child is of course beautiful. (Luke 2:40.) In *Plate 33,* the artist has emphasized the last phrase of Luke 2:40, "The grace of God was upon him." The Father in heaven is visibly present, and the grace descends upon the child in the form of a dove, as suggested by Luke 3:22. The action of all the accessory figures, the arrangement of the light, everything in the picture, is calculated to focus the attention upon the face of the child Christ.

[Illustration: Madonna and Child.] Plate 32. *Madonna and Child.* Murillo. 1618-1682.

[Illustration: Holy Family.] Plate 33. Louvre. *Holy Family.* Murillo. 1618-1682.

Hofmann, Plate 31, tells of the quiet days at Nazareth, when Joseph worked at his trade, and Mary sat near spinning and watching the wondrous lad who in his child-way could help Joseph by fetching a needed tool. It was a peaceful, happy life, like that of the chickens and the doves. The memories of those days furnished Jesus with the wonderful figure of speech recorded in Matt. 23:37, 38. Hofmann, like other artists, is fond of symbolism, hence the square and the measuring stick are upon the shoulder of the child (Is. 9:6) who was to lay judgment to the line and righteousness to the plummet (Is. 28:17); and the tools take the form of the cross. Jesus was subject unto his parents (Luke 2:51), and, in a sense, took up his cross daily, as all his disciples must ever do (Matt. 16:24). Such service is healthful and profitable (Luke 2:52).

[Illustration: Infancy of Christ.] Plate 31. *Infancy of Christ.* H. Hofmann. 1824-

THE VISIT TO JERUSALEM.

Joseph and Mary probably went every year to Jerusalem at the feast of the passover. (Deut. 16:16.) And when Jesus was twelve years old they went up as usual taking him with them. (Luke 2:41-42.)

Mengelberg, Plate 34, represents the holy family approaching the city. The temple with its smoking altars is seen in the distance. The artist has suggested the great company who went up every year to worship, and with which, returning, Joseph and Mary supposed Jesus to be.

[Illustration: Jesus, Twelve Years Old, on his way to Jerusalem.] Plate 34. *Jesus, Twelve Years Old, on his Way to Jerusalem.* O. Mengelberg.

Hofmann, Plates 38 and 39, illustrates (Luke 2:46). Plate 38 is from the drawing in the artist's Life of Christ. Plate 39, from the famous painting in Dresden, is the more carefully finished. Hofmann has shown the seal of Solomon upon the "chair of philosophy," he has introduced the scroll of the prophets and suggested the rich stones of the temple, but the interest of all is upon the Boy, who came to fulfill the law and the prophets, and who was greater than the temple and greater than Solomon. (Matt. 5:17, John 2:19-20, Matt. 12:42). This picture has become a classic already, though Hofmann is still living.

[Illustration: Christ Disputing with the Doctors.] Plate 38. *Christ Disputing with the Doctors.* H. Hofmann. 1824-

[Illustration: In The Temple.] Plate 39. *In The Temple.* H. Hofmann. 1824-

Lafon, Plate 36, has idealized his subject. He has placed Jesus "in Moses' seat" (Matt. 23:2), conferring upon him a distinction amply justified by subsequent events especially by the Sermon on the Mount. "It hath been said . . . but I say unto you . . ." these are the words which give Jesus a unique position as a teacher.

[Illustration: Christ Among the Doctors.] Plate 36. *Christ Among the Doctors.* Émile J. Lafon.

Hunt, Plate 35, adds that truthfulness of detail, that literalness of statement made possible by the antiquarian and the archæologist. It is the moment described in Luke 2:48, when his mother speaks to Jesus,

"Son, why hast thou dealt thus with us?"

[Illustration: Finding of Christ in the Temple.] Plate 35. *Finding of Christ in the Temple.* Holman Hunt. 1827-

Dobson, Plate 37, shows the moment of discovery, the moment just before Mary speaks. Some of the kinsfolk and acquaintances have evidently returned with Joseph and Mary. A rabbi is telling them about this wondrous child. (Luke 2:47.)

[Illustration: Christ Disputing in the Temple.] Plate 37. *Christ Disputing in the Temple.* W. C. T. Dobson.

THE SILENT YEARS AT HOME.

Tradition says that Joseph soon died, and that Jesus supported the family by working at his trade.

Hunt, Plate 40, has invented an occasion to emphasize the prophetic words often applied to Mary, "Is any sorrow like unto my sorrow?" (Lam. 1:12.) Simeon had said "Yea and a sword shall pierce through thine own soul," and Mary, "pondering all these things in her heart," is startled, at the close of the day, by seeing the shadow of her son cast upon the wall, like the form of one upon a cross.

[Illustration: Shadow of Death.] Plate 40. *Shadow of Death.* Holman Hunt. 1827-

Plockhörst, Plate 41, depicts the parting of Mother and Son,-- another pang for the saintly Mary.

[Illustration: Christ taking leave of his Mother.] Plate 41. *Christ taking leave of his Mother.* B. Plockhörst. 1825-

Plate 42 is Andrea del Sarto's famous the youthful John the Baptist, in the days before he came preaching in the of Judea. (Luke 1:80.)

[Illustration: John the Baptist.] Plate 42. *John the Baptist.* Andrea del Sarto. 1488-1530.

Titian, Plate 43, shows John as he appeared a few years later upon the banks of Jordan, "his raiment of camel's hair, and a leathern girdle about his loins." (Matt. 3:1-4.) He seems to be saying, "Behold the Lamb of God, which taketh away the sin of the world." (John 1:29.) The river is introduced as a symbol (Luke 3:16), and the lamb also (John 1:35). Del Sarto seems to have studied this figure before painting his boy John. Compare the two faces, and the two arms and hands. Notice the two crosses also.

[Illustration: John the Baptist Preaching.] Plate 43. *John the Baptist Preaching.* Titian. 1477-1576.

THE TEMPTATION.

Scheffer, Plate 44, shows Jesus "upon an exceeding high mountain" and Satan offering him the world for one act of worship. Jesus is about to say, "Worship God." (Matt. 4:8-10.) *Hofmann, Plate 45,* has selected the next moment when Satan retreats and an angel comes to minister to the famished man. (Matt. 4:11.) The serpent is present because of Rev. 12:9.

[Illustration: Temptation of Christ.] Plate 44. *Temptation of Christ.* Ary Scheffer. 1795-1858.

[Illustration: Temptation.] Plate 45. *Temptation.* H. Hofmann. 1824-

THE BEGINNING OF PUBLIC SERVICE.

Bida, Plate 46, illustrates John 1:35. "Behold the Lamb of God," said John to two of his disciples, who straightway left John and followed Jesus. *Grünewald, Plate 48,* represents Jesus meditating as he walks by the sea alone, possibly before he had chosen his disciples, but more likely after the people threatened to make him a King (John 6:15), for it is evening near the sea of Galilee.

[Illustration: Behold the Lamb of God.] Plate 46. *Behold the Lamb of God.* Alexandre Bida. 1813-1895.

[Illustration: Jesus Walking by the Sea.] Plate 48. *Jesus Walking by the Sea*. M. Grünewald (was painting 1518).

Veronese, Plate 50, transforms the modest wedding at Cana into a gorgeous Venetian Feast, to which "Jesus also was bidden, and his disciples," "and the Mother of Jesus was there." (John 2:1-2.) They may all be discovered in the central part of the picture, but to the mind of Veronese the miracle of the wine seems to be of but secondary importance.

[Illustration: The Marriage Feast.] Plate 50. *The Marriage Feast*. Paolo Veronese. 1528-1588.

EARLY JUDEAN MINISTRY.

Kirchbuck, Plate 51, presents a general view of the event recorded in John 2:13-22. Jesus expels the desecrators by his presence merely, as he overthrew his enemies in Gethsemane. (John 18:6.)

[Illustration: Christ casting out the Money-changers.] Plate 51. *Christ casting out the Money-changers*. F. Kirchbuck.

Hofmann, Plate 52, with his usual literalness, gives Jesus the whip of small cords, and represents him as actively aggressive. "The zeal of thine house shall eat me up," said the prophet, and as they watched Jesus the disciples remembered those words. (John 2:17.)

[Illustration: Purification of the Temple.] Plate 52. *Purification of the Temple*. H. Hofmann. 1824-

Plate 53, by an unknown artist, is an attempt to portray the discourse with Nicodemus. The incident is related in John 2:23-3:21. The moment is that when Jesus says, "If I have told you earthly things and ye believe not, how shall ye believe if I tell you heavenly things?"

[Illustration: Nicodemus' Visit to Jesus.] Plate 53. *Nicodemus' Visit to Jesus*. Artist unknown.

THE RETURN THROUGH SAMARIA.

"He came to a town called Shechem, near the plot of land that Jacob gave his son Joseph. Jacob's Spring was there, and Jesus, being tired after his journey, sat down, just as he was, close to it. It was then about mid-day. A woman of Samaria came to draw water; so Jesus asked her to give him some to drink, his disciples having gone into the town to buy provisions." [*]

[*] Twentieth Century New Testament

Biliverti, Plate 56, gives the woman a companion not mentioned in the text. The moment is that of John 4:10, "If you knew the gift of God, and who it is that is asking you to give him some water, you would have asked him, and he would have given you living water."

[Illustration: Jesus and the Woman of Samaria.] Plate 56. *Jesus and the Woman of Samaria.* Biliverti.

Doré, Plate 54, has selected a later moment, "Trust me," Jesus replied, "a time is coming when it will not be on this mountain or in Jerusalem that you will worship God the Father."

[Illustration: Jesus and the Woman of Samaria.] Plate 54. *Jesus and the Woman of Samaria.* Gustave Doré. 1833-1883.

Hofmann, Plate 55, may have chosen to illustrate the twenty-fourth verse, "God is Spirit; and those who worship him must worship spiritually, with true insight." (John 4:24.)

[Illustration: Jesus and the Woman of Samaria.] Plate 55. *Jesus and the Woman of Samaria.* H. Hofmann. 1824-

THE CALL OF THE FOUR.

Walking by the sea of Galilee one morning, Jesus saw two brethren, Simon who is called Peter, and Andrew his brother, . . . and two other brethren, James, the son of Zebedee, and John his brother, with their nets, for they were fishermen. And he called them: "Come ye after me and I will make you fishers of men." These four became his first disciples. (Matt. 4:18-22.)

Zimmermann, Plate 47, has seized upon the moment when Jesus makes that extraordinary statement. Peter and John are nearest Jesus, the other two in the background. "Fishers of men;" the phrase is mysterious; they cannot understand it. Nevertheless, they leave all and follow Him.

[Illustration: Christ and the Fishermen.] Plate 47. *Christ and the Fishermen.* Zimmermann. 1832-

Luke gives the account of a miracle between the morning sermon of Jesus to the crowd upon the beach, and this call of the four fishermen: "When he had finished speaking he said to Simon, Push off into deep water, and then all throw out your nets for a haul." "We have been hard at work all night, sir," Simon answered, "and have not caught anything, but as you say so, I will throw the nets out." They did so, and they enclosed such a great shoal of fish that their nets began to break. So they signalled to their mates in the other boat to come and help them; which they did, filling both the boats so full of fish that they were almost sinking.

Raphael, Plate 49, illustrates the moment, a little later, when Peter threw himself down at Jesus' knees, exclaiming: "Depart from me, for I am a sinful man, O Lord." (Luke 5:8.) Raphael made this as a design for a tapestry for the Sistine Chapel, Rome.

[Illustration: The Miraculous Draught of Fishes.] Plate 49. *The Miraculous Draught of Fishes.* Raphael. 1483-1520.

EARLY GALILEAN MINISTRY.

Schönherr, Plate 69, Hofmann, Plate 70, Max, Plate 71, give different interpretations of Matt. 8:16-17. An evening at Capernaum, when the words of Isaiah (53:4) began to be fulfilled, "Himself took our infirmities and bare our diseases."

[Illustration: Healing the Sick.] Plate 69. *Healing the Sick.* Karl Gottlieb Schönherr. 1824-

[Illustration: Healing the Sick.] Plate 70. *Healing the Sick.* H. Hofmann. 1824-

[Illustration: Healing the Sick Child.] Plate 71. *Healing the Sick Child.* Gabriel Max. 1840-

The Call of Matthew has been represented variously. (Matt. 9:9-10.)

Pordenone, Plate 59, has Matthew "sitting at the place of toll."

[Illustration: Calling of Matthew.] Plate 59. *Calling of Matthew.* Giovanni Pordenone. 1483-1539.

Bida, Plate 57, shows Jesus "as he passed by," and Matthew leaving his place of business to follow him.

[Illustration: Calling of Matthew.] Plate 57. *Calling of Matthew.* Alexandre Bida. 1813-1895.

Chimenti, Plate 58, would have us believe that Jesus entered the great khan of the city where the customs were collected, and called Matthew from thence.

[Illustration: Calling of Matthew.] Place 58. *Calling of Matthew.* Jacopo Chimenti.

AT JERUSALEM AGAIN.

After these things Jesus went up to Jerusalem to a Feast of the Jews, and visited the Pool of Bethesda. There he saw a man who had been infirm for thirty-eight years. After talking with him Jesus cured him, although it was Sabbath. (John 5:1-8.)

Van Lint, Plate 61, shows the man arising with his bed, verse 9.

[Illustration: Healing of the Impotent Man.] Plate 61. *Healing of the Impotent Man.* Peter Van Lint.

Bida, Plate 60, represents the instant when Jesus is giving the command, but before the man has grasped its meaning. Both artists suggest the pool, with its colonnade, or porches. Perhaps a subsequent event is illustrated by *Van Dyck, Plate 62,* for "Afterward Jesus findeth him in the temple, and said unto him, Behold thou art made whole; sin no more lest a worse thing befall thee." (John 5:14.)

[Illustration: Healing of the Impotent Man.] Plate 60. *Healing of the Impotent Man.* Alexandra Bida. 1813-1895.

[Illustration: Talking with the Lame Man, Bethesda.] Plate 62. *Talking with the Lame Man, Bethesda.* Van Dyck. 1599-1641.

Doré, Plate 63, gives an interpretation of Matt. 12:1-8. The Pharisees are accusing the disciples of breaking the Sabbath by plucking the heads of wheat, and Jesus is excusing them. The Master seems to be saying, "Have ye not read what David did when he was an hungered, and they that were with him? . . . If ye had known ye would not have condemned the guiltless. The Son of man is lord of the Sabbath. The Sabbath was made for man, not man for the Sabbath." (Mark 2:27.)

[Illustration: Jesus and His Disciples Going Through the Cornfield.] Plate 63. *Jesus and His Disciples Going Through the Cornfield.* Gustave Doré. 1833-1883.

THE SERMON ON THE MOUNT

"And seeing the multitudes, he went up into the mountain, and when he had sat down, his disciples came unto him, and he opened his mouth and taught them." (Matt. 5:1, 2.)

Doré, Plate 65, has represented the scene as a whole. The instant might be almost any in the discourse.

[Illustration: The Sermon on the Mount.] Plate 65. *The Sermon on the Mount.* Gustave Doré. 1833-1883.

Hofmann, Plate 64, seems to have depicted the giving of the beatitudes. The poor in spirit, the mourner, the meek, those who hunger for righteousness, the pure, and the persecuted, all seem to be represented in the audience.

[Illustration: The Sermon on the Mount.] Plate 64. *The Sermon on the Mount.* H. Hofmann. 1824-

Jeune, Plate 67, has selected the moment when Jesus says, "Consider the lilies how they grow. . . . If God so clothe the grass of the field, shall he not much more clothe you? . . . Seek first his kingdom and his righteousness." (Matt. 6:28-33.)

[Illustration: Consider the Lilies.] Plate 67. *Consider the Lilies.* Henry Le Jeune. 1820.

Bida, Plate 66, illustrates one section of the Sermon on the Mount, viz.: Matt. 6:5-15. Here is the man in his inner chamber, having shut his door, praying to his Father who is in secret, and who will reward him.

[Illustration: Prayer in Secret.] Plate 66. *Prayer in Secret.* Alexandra Bida. 1813-1895.

EVENTS DURING THE SECOND TOUR OF GALILEE.

Veronese, Plate 68, represents the Centurion who came to Jesus at Capernaum, beseeching him to cure his servant. "I am not worthy," the Centurion is saying, "that thou shouldest come under my roof--only say the word and my servant shall be healed." (Matt. 8:8.)

[Illustration: The Centurion's Servant.] Plate 68. *The Centurion's Servant.* Veronese. 1528-1588.

Hofmann, Plate 72, has illustrated the raising of the widow of Nain's son, as graphically as Luke has told it, in chapter 7, verses 11 to 16. "Every one was awe-struck and began praising God."

[Illustration: Raising the Widow's Son.] Plate 72. *Raising the Widow's Son.* H. Hofmann. 1824-

Veronese, Plate 73, gives another grand feast to his friends (compare plate 50). This time it is supposed to be in the house of Simon the Pharisee, as recorded in Luke 7:36-50. The woman, who bathed the Master's feet with tears, is in this case a beautiful and decorous person, a center of attraction.

[Illustration: Jesus in the House of Simon.] Plate 73. *Jesus in the House of Simon.* Paolo Veronese. 1528-1588.

Rubens, Plate 74, has been more faithful to the story as recorded. The woman kisses the Master's feet and wipes them with her hair, v. 38. There is great consternation among the guests.

[Illustration: Magdalen.] Plate 74. *Magdalen.* Rubens. 1577-1640.

Hofmann, Plate 75, shows the self-righteous Pharisee, with his hypocritical friends, more graphically than either of the other artists. His keen insight into character is reflected from every face. Hofmann, above many others, is true to the account, and true to human nature. "Thy sins are forgiven," Jesus is saying. (Verse 48.)

[Illustration: Anointing Feet of Jesus.] Plate 75. *Anointing Feet of Jesus.* H. Hofmann. 1824-

Hofmann, Plate 76, tells of Jesus preaching from the boat (Mark 4:1). Every face in the picture is worth studying. The world is present by representation--infancy, childhood, youth, maturity, old age; the healthy and the diseased, the workman and the scholar. "And he taught them many things in parables," among other things the truth about the Kingdom of God. (Luke 8:9-10.)

[Illustration: Jesus Preaches from a Boat.] Plate 76. *Jesus Preaches from a Boat.* H. Hofmann. 1824-

Robert, Plate 77, in four decorative panels, illustrates the parable of the Sower, which Jesus gave at this time. In the first the birds came and devoured the seed, in the second the stony ground offered no good opportunity for a harvest, in the third thorns and thistles and other worldly things, "the deceitfulness of riches and the lusts of other things," symbolized by the short-lived mushrooms and daisies, and by the moths, choke the good seed. In the last is the abundant harvest. (Mark 4:1-34.)

[Illustration: Parable of the Sower.] Plate 77. *Parable of the Sower.* H. L. Robert

And when Jesus had finished these parables he departed to the other side of the lake. "And behold there arose a great tempest in the sea." *Doré, Plate 78,* shows the disciples in fear, crying out, "Save, Lord; we perish." Jesus, awakened from a sound sleep, says calmly, "Why are ye fearful, O ye of little faith?" (Matt. 8:25-26.) "Then he arose and rebuked the winds and the sea, and there was a great calm." (Verse 26.)

[Illustration: "Peace, Be Still."] Plate 78. *"Peace, Be Still."* Gustave Doré. 1833-1883.

By the time Jesus had re-crossed in the boat, a great number of people had gathered to meet him. Here Jairus came and entreated Jesus to cure his little daughter who was at the point of death. As they were going to the house, servants came saying that the child was dead: but they went on to the house of Jairus. Clearing the house of the mourners, Jesus takes the child's father and mother, Peter, James and John, and with them enters the room of death. (Mark 5:21, 24, 35-40.)

Richter, Plate 80, is true to the account in the number of witnesses, but not in the action of the Master.

[Illustration: Christ Raising the Daughter of Jairus.] Plate 80. *Christ Raising the Daughter of Jairus.* Gustav Richter. 1823-1884.

Hofmann, Plate 79, is, as usual, more literal. "Taking the child by the hand" Jesus said, "Little girl, I am speaking to you, get up." (Mark 5:41.)

[Illustration: Daughter of Jairus.] Plate 79. *Daughter of Jairus.* H. Hofmann. 1824-

Keller, Plate 81, shows the next moment when the damsel arose and the people were "utterly astounded." (Verse 43 in Twentieth Century New Testament.) Keller is no doubt more accurate than either of the others in the matters of costume and other accessories. The face of the child is worth studying.

[Illustration: Raising the Daughter of Jairus.] Plate 81. *Raising the Daughter of Jairus.* A. Keller.

DEATH OF JOHN THE BAPTIST.

The account is given in Mark 6:14-29.

Reni, Plate 82, represents the daughter of Herodius bearing John's head to her mother. At Herod's command a soldier had brought it in a charger, and given it to the damsel. (Verse 28.)

[Illustration: Head of John the Baptist in a Charger.] Plate 82. *Head of John the Baptist in a Charger.* Guido Reni. 1575- 1642.

THE FEEDING OF THE FIVE THOUSAND.

When Jesus heard of the death of John he withdrew into a desert place to rest. But the crowds followed him on foot from all the cities of Galilee. After a day spent in healing the sick and in teaching, the Master fed the multitude generously, with five loaves and two fishes. The account is given by Mark (6:30-46) and by all the other evangelists.

Murillo, Plate 83, has selected the moment when the multitude is being seated "by companies upon the green grass," and the disciples are procuring the loaves and fishes from the lad. (John 6:9.) Jesus is taking the loaves preparatory to giving thanks and distributing them.

[Illustration: Miracle of the Loaves and Fishes.] Plate 83. *Miracle of the Loaves and Fishes.* Bartolome Esteran Murillo. 1618-1682.

The following night Jesus came to the disciples, walking upon the water. The most complete account is given by Matthew (14:24-36).

Upon Peter's request Jesus gave him permission to come out upon the water.

Schwartz, Plate 85, shows the moment when Peter, sinking, cries out, "Lord, save me." (Matt. 14:30.)

[Illustration: Christ and St. Peter.] Plate 85. *Christ and St. Peter.* A. Schwartz.

Plockhörst, Plate 84, gives the next instant when Jesus stretched forth his hand and took hold of him, saying, "O thou of little faith, wherefore didst thou doubt?" (Matt. 14:31.)

[Illustration: Christ and St. Peter.] Plate 84. *Christ and St. Peter.* S. Plockhörst. 1825-

THE TRIP INTO PHOENICIA.

And Jesus went away into the borders of Tyre and Sidon. There a Canaanitish woman begged him to cure her daughter. The interesting dialogue which ensued is recorded by both Matthew and Mark.

Vecchio, Plate 86, gives the beginning of the dialogue. "I was not sent but unto the lost sheep of the house of Israel." (Matt. 15:24.)

[Illustration: The Canaanitish Woman.] Plate 86. *The Canaanitish Woman.* Palma Vecchio. 1475-1528.

PETER'S CONFESSION.

The event recorded in Matt. 16:13-20, and that recorded in John 21:15-23, have often been closely related in the minds of artists employed by the church during the middle ages.

Reni, Plate 87, gives a literal interpretation to Matt. 16:19. "I give unto thee the keys of the kingdom of heaven."

[Illustration: Christ Giving Keys to St. Peter.] Plate 87. *Christ Giving Keys to St. Peter.* Guido Reni. 1575-1642.

Raphael, Plate 88, represents the later event, when Christ says, "Feed my sheep," but Peter has evidently just received the keys. The sheep are actually present, as symbols, to make clear the moment selected by the artist. (John 21:17.)

[Illustration: Christ's Charge to St. Peter.] Plate 88. *Christ's Charge to St. Peter.* Raphael. 1483-1520.

THE TRANSFIGURATION.

Raphael, Plate 89, has given upon one canvas, and that one of the most famous in the world, the Transfiguration, and that which took place at the same time at the foot of the mountain. (Luke 9:28-36, and Mark 9:14-29.) *Plate 90* is a part of the same picture. Compare the details of both of these plates with the scriptural account! No artist ever packed more literal and spiritual truth into a single canvas.

[Illustration: The Transfiguration.] Plate 89. *The Transfiguration.* Raphael. 1483-1520.

[Illustration: The Demoniac Boy.] Plate 90. *The Demoniac Boy.* Raphael. 1483-1520.

Shortly after the Transfiguration Jesus talked with his disciples about true greatness. By way of illustration "He took a little child in his arms and said unto them, Whosoever shall humble himself as this little child, the same is the greatest in the kingdom of heaven." (Mark 9:36, Matt. 18:4.)

Ballheim, Plate 97, suggests this event.

[Illustration: Jesus and the Child.] Plate 97. *Jesus and the Child.* H. Ballheim.

AT THE FEAST OF TABERNACLES.

The Scribes and the Pharisees brought to Jesus a woman taken in adultery.

Hofmann, Plate 91, depicts the scene most graphically, at the moment when Jesus says, "Let him that is without sin cast the first stone."

[Illustration: Christ and the Sinner.] Plate 91. *Christ and the Sinner.* H. Hofmann. 1824-

Signol, Plate 92, does not show the woman "in the midst" as did Hofmann, but after they had gone out one by one, when Jesus was left alone with the woman. The words, "Let him that is without sin," etc., are written upon the pavement because of verses 6 and 8, where it is said that Jesus wrote upon the ground.

[Illustration: The Adulterous Woman.] Plate 92. *The Adulterous Woman.* Emile Signol.

At this feast Jesus spoke of himself as the Light of the world. (John 8:12-30.)

Hunt, Plate 93, has idealized the words of Jesus, and added the thought expressed in Rev. 3:20, "Behold, I stand at the door and knock." The picture shows also, without doubt, the influence of the well-known hymn, by Mrs. Stowe, "Knocking, knocking, who is there?" Every detail of this picture is symbolical, and most exquisitely painted.

[Illustration: "I am the Light of the World."] Plate 93. *"I am the Light of the World."* Holman Hunt. 1827-

Overbeck, Plate 94, emphasizes the thought in Rev. 3:20.

[Illustration: "Behold, I stand at the Door and Knock."] Plate 94. *"Behold, I stand at the Door and Knock."* Overbeck. 1789- 1869.

Plockhörst, Plate 99, has attempted to put into a single picture the wealth of meaning suggested by the wondrous words, "Come unto me, all ye that labor and are heavy laden, and I will give you rest." (Matt, 11:28.) Humanity is symbolized by the pilgrim who needs comforting.

[Illustration: Christ the Consoler.] Plate 99. *Christ the Consoler.* B. Plockhörst. 1825-

THE PEREAN MINISTRY.

During this part of his life Jesus gave some of his most famous parables.

Siemenroth, Plate 101, illustrates the parable of the Good Samaritan. The Priest and the Levite have passed by; the Samaritan is pouring oil and wine upon the wounds preparatory to binding them up. (Luke 10:30-34.)

[Illustration: The Good Samaritan.] Plate 101. *The Good Samaritan.* K. Siemenroth.

Doré, Plate 100, shows the Samaritan bringing the wounded man to the inn, as described in verse 34. In both pictures the plains of Jericho are shown in the distance. It is interesting to note that one artist translates "beast" as an ass, and the other as a horse.

[Illustration: The Good Samaritan.] Plate 100. *The Good Samaritan.* Gustave Doré. 1833-1883.

The Perean ministry was interrupted by a visit to Bethany and Jerusalem.

Hofmann, Plate 114, has most beautifully drawn the group in the home of Lazarus,--Martha, "cumbered with much serving," (Luke 10:40), Mary, "who has chosen the good part," (verse 40), and for a reminder of Lazarus, who has not yet returned from work, his house-dog, asleep by the chair of Jesus.

[Illustration: Bethany.] Plate 114. *Bethany.* H. Hofmann. 1824-

Allori, Plate 113, gives Martha a maidservant drawing water, and a man-servant bringing in a sheep for dinner. Mary has her alabaster box close at hand! (Compare John 12:1-3.) About the time of the visit Jesus opened the eyes of the man born blind. (John 9.)

[Illustration: Christ in the House of Mary and Martha.] Plate 113. *Christ in the House of Mary and Martha.* A. Allori. 1544- 1628.

Theotocopuli, Plate 115, represents Jesus performing the miracle, and the hypocritical Pharisees, shocked and offended that he should do such a thing on the Sabbath. Following this event was the discourse about "The Good Shepherd." (John 10:1-21.)

[Illustration: Jesus Anoints the Blind Man's Eyes with Clay.] Plate 115. *Jesus Anoints the Blind Man's Eyes with Clay.* Theotocopuli. 1548-1625.

Plockhörst, Plate 116, has chosen to illustrate the phrase, "He goeth before them and the sheep follow him."

Upon returning into Perea Jesus gave the "Three Parables of Grace." (Luke 15.)

[Illustration: The Good Shepherd.] Plate 116. *The Good Shepherd.* B. Plockhörst. 1825-

Schönherr, Plate 117, and *Molitor, Plate 102,* represent the good shepherd who leaves the ninety and nine on the moor and goes after the lost sheep until he finds it. (Luke 15:4.)

[Illustration: The Good Shepherd.] Plate 117. The Good Shepherd. Carl Schönherr.

[Illustration: The Lost Sheep.] Plate 102. *The Lost Sheep.* Franz Molitor.

Millais, Plate 103, illustrates the next parable, that of the lost coin. "If a woman lose a coin, does she not light a candle and search carefully until she finds it?" (Luke 15:8-10.)

[Illustration: The Lost Piece of Money.] Plate 103. *The Lost Piece of Money.* Sir John Millais. 1829-1896.

If the first parable of the group teaches the compassion of the Son, and the second the solicitude of the Spirit, the third teaches the enduring love of God the Father.

Molitor, Plate 105, has designed an almost abstract father and son--*a* prodigal, perhaps, but not *the* prodigal--to match his panel of the lost sheep. The parable is but faintly echoed in this picture.

[Illustration: Prodigal Son.] Plate 105. *Prodigal Son.* Franz Molitor.

The man who has painted the parable as a whole is *Dubufe, Plate 106.* The central panel in the triptych shows the young man wasting his substance in riotous living. "He squandered his property by his dissolute life," says one version. His feasts were such as that described by Isaiah 5:11, 12. The panel at the left shows the young man in want, feeding swine, when "no man gave unto him." (Luke 15:16.) In that at the right, he has returned to his father's house.

[Illustration: The Prodigal Son.] Plate 106. *The Prodigal Son.* E. Dubufe.

Doré, Plate 104, is truer to the parable in the matter of the return, for "while he was yet a great way off his father saw him and ran, and fell on his neck and kissed him." (Luke 15:20.)

[Illustration: Prodigal Son.] Plate 104. *Prodigal Son.* Gustave Doré. 1833-1883.

Doré, Plate 107, illustrates the parable of the Rich Man and Lazarus, as recorded in Luke 16:19-31. He has added a dramatic touch by representing the servants ordering the beggar away, even with violence--a part of the "evil things" which Lazarus received during his life. (Luke 16:25.)

[Illustration: The Rich Man and Lazarus.] Plate 107. *The Rich Man and Lazarus.* Gustave Doré. 1833-1883.

Jesus was again called to visit Bethany by the death of the brother of Mary and Martha. None of the pictures here reproduced give an adequate representation of that which then occurred--the raising of Lazurus. Perhaps the event is too august to be put upon canvas.

Bonifazio, Plate 118, seems to take an almost childish delight in depicting the varying effects of a disagreeable odor! He has magnified the remark of Martha (John 11:39) into the motive for a picture!

[Illustration: Raising of Lazarus.] Plate 118. *Raising of Lazarus.* Bonifazio II. 1494-1563.

Piombo, Plate 119, suggests the large company who witnessed the miracle, but ignores the statement that Lazarus was buried in a cave, and that he came forth without assistance. (Verses 38 and 44.) He has surpassed Bonifazio in one respect at least. Piombo's people are astonished and excited over what has occurred: they are not entirely witless because of Martha's suggestion.

[Illustration: Raising of Lazarus.] Plate 119. *Raising of Lazarus.* Sebastian del Piombo. 1485-1547.

Rubens, Plate 120, has not included the crowd in his canvas; but his Lazarus comes forth vigorously and happily from his grave in the cave, to meet a master whose figure is charged with animation. The traditional characters of the sisters are not forgotten. Martha helps to remove the grave-clothes, while Mary, as usual, worships the Master.

[Illustration: Raising of Lazarus.] Plate 120. *Raising of Lazarus.* Rubens. 1577-1640.

Doré, Plate 108, interprets the parable of the Pharisee and the Publican. The Pharisee stands and prays "with himself" (Luke 18:11), while the tax-gatherer will not so much as "lift up his eyes to heaven," but says, "God be merciful to me a sinner." (Verse 13.) Jesus is represented as saying, "This man went down to his house justified." (Verse 14.) Doré makes it an actual event, not merely a parable.

[Illustration: The Pharisee and Publican.] Plate 108. *The Pharisee and Publican.* Gustave Doré. 1833-1883.

Christ blessing the children, has been a favorite subject with artists.

Hofmann, Plate 109, tells the story in his own charming way. How sweetly child-like is that offering of the little bouquet! He remembers that not only little children came; mothers brought their babies. (Luke 18:15.)

[Illustration: Christ Blessing Little Children.] Plate 109. *Christ Blessing Little Children.* H. Hofmann. 1824-

Plockhörst, Plate 110, is equally true to the account and to nature. Here a little child is asking to take her flowers to Jesus. Plockhörst loves symbolism. Sheep are present (Is. 40:11), and a little boy is about to offer Jesus a palm-branch in unconscious anticipation of his triumphal entry to Jerusalem. (Matt. 21:8, 9 and 15.)

[Illustration: Christ Blessing Little Children.] Plate 110. *Christ Blessing Little Children.* B. Plockhörst. 1825-

Vogel, Plate 111, has introduced one or two children old enough to have some consciousness of a real need of such love and forgiveness as the Master offers to all. Their attitude is not that of naïve childhood.

[Illustration: Christ Blessing Little Children.] Plate 111. *Christ Blessing Little Children.* Carlo Vogel.

Hofmann, Plate 112, has excelled himself in the portrayal of Christ and the rich young ruler, who asked how to obtain eternal life. (Matt. 19:16.) Jesus is saying; "If thou wouldest be perfect go sell what thou hast and give to the poor, and thou shalt have treasure in heaven." The decision of the young man is already made. He will presently go away sorrowful, and keep his great possessions. (Matt. 19:21, 22.)

[Illustration: Christ and the Young Ruler.] Plate 112. *Christ and the Young Ruler.* H. Hofmann. 1824-

Bonifazio, Plate 121, illustrates the account of Matthew relative to the ambitions of James and John.

Their mother comes worshiping, and asking that her two sons may receive special honor in Christ's Kingdom. Jesus is saying, "My cup indeed ye shall drink; but to sit on my right hand and on my left hand it is not mine to give." (Matt. 20:20-28.) Peter is ready to add his word of condemnation.

[Illustration: Christ and Zebedee's Children.] Plate 121. *Christ and Zebedee's Children.* Bonifazio. 1494-1563.

AT JERUSALEM.

PASSION WEEK.

Jesus went on his way towards Jerusalem, and when he came within sight of the city he wept over it and said, "Would that you had learned, while there was time--yes, even you--the things that make for peace! But as it is, they have been hidden from your sight. For a time is coming for you when your enemies will surround you with earthworks, and encircle you, and hem you in on every side; they will trample you down and your children within you, and they will not leave in you one stone upon another, because you did not see that God was visiting you." (Twentieth Century N. T., Luke 19:42-44.)

Eastlake, Plate, 124, has not followed the scriptural account closely, but has designed a panel, with the text in mind, possibly influenced also by Matt. 23:37, "How often would I have gathered thy children together as a hen gathers her chickens under her wings, and ye would not!"

[Illustration: Christ Weeps Over Jerusalem.] Plate 124. *Christ Weeps Over Jerusalem.* Sir Charles Eastlake. 1793- 1865.

Deger, Plate 123, represents the triumphal entry into Jerusalem as recorded in all the Gospels, but with most complete detail in Luke 19:29-44. The people threw their garments upon a colt, and set Jesus thereon, and accompanied him from Bethpage to Jerusalem, waving palm branches (John 12:13), and spreading garments and palms in the street (Matt. 21:8), and shouting "Hosanna, Blessed is he that cometh in the name of the Lord." (Matt. 21:9.) The artist has allowed the mother of Jesus to witness this short lived triumph of her son; nor has he forgotten the children (Matt. 21:15).

[Illustration: Triumphal Entry.] Plate 123. *Triumphal Entry.* Ernest Deger. 1809-1885.

Doré, Plates 125 and 127, gives two incidents of the early part of the week: the Herodians asking about tribute to Cæsar (Matt. 22:16- 22), and the poor widow giving her contribution to the temple treasury (Mark 12:41-44).

[Illustration: Jesus and the Tribute Money.] Plate 125. *Jesus and the Tribute Money.* Gustave Doré. 1833-1883.

[Illustration: The Widow's Mite.] Plate 127. *The Widow's Mite.* Gustave Doré. 1833-1883.

Titian, Plate 126, in dealing with the incident of the tribute to Cæsar, has selected the moment Doré selected, when Jesus asks, "Whose image and superscription hath it?" (Mark 20:24.)

[Illustration: Tribute to Cæsar.] Plate 126. *Tribute to Cæsar.* Titian. 1477-1576.

Van Dyck, Plate 96, has chosen the moment when Jesus says, "Render therefore unto Cæsar the things that are Cæsar's, and unto God the things that are God's" (Matt. 22:21).

[Illustration: Tribute Money.] Plate 96. *Tribute Money.* A. Van Dyck. 1599-1641.

Towards the close of his discourse about The Last Things, Jesus gave the parable of the Wise and Foolish Virgins. (Matt. 25:1-13.)

Poloty, Plate 128, has attempted to illustrate this parable, and has chosen the moment when the foolish virgins discover that they are unprepared. (Verses 8 and 9.) Evidently the cry, "Behold the bridegroom cometh," was not heard, upon this occasion, "at midnight" (Verse 6.)

[Illustration: Parable of the Virgins.] Plate 128. *Parable of the Virgins.* Carl Theodor von Poloty. 1826- 1886.

THE LAST SUPPER.

[Illustration: Conspiracy Against Jesus.] Plate 129. *Conspiracy Against Jesus.* Alexandre Bida. 1813-1895.

When the disciples entered the upper room all had neglected to assume the office of servant in preparation for the meal. They were disputing as to who should be the greatest in the kingdom. (Luke 22:24.) Jesus therefore arose from the table and performed the act of cleansing.

Brown, Plate 133, has portrayed the incident wonderfully well. The dialogue with Peter is just finished. (John 13:6-10.)

[Illustration: Jesus Washes the Disciples' Feet.] Plate 133. *Jesus Washes the Disciples' Feet.* Ford Madox Brown. 1821-1893.

Da Vinci, Plate 131, has excelled all others in rendering the effects of the announcement Jesus made shortly afterwards, when they were at table again, "One of you shall betray me." Some of the disciples wonder (John 13:22), some ask, "Is it I?" (Mark 14:19.) Peter whispers to John to inquire who it is. (John 13:24.) The face of Judas alone is in shadow and inscrutable. Presently Judas will go out to the conspiring chief priests. (John 13:27-30.)

[Illustration: The Last Supper.] Plate 131. *The Last Supper.* Leonardo Da Vinci. 1452-1519.

When Judas had departed, Jesus said, "Now is the Son of man glorified." (John 13:31.) "And as they were eating, Jesus took bread and blessed, and break it."

Bida, Plate 132, gives a graphic picture of the moment of blessing the bread. "This is my body which is given for you," he said (Luke 22:19). "This do in remembrance of me."

[Illustration: The Last Supper.] Plate 132. *The Last Supper.* Alexandra Bida. 1813-1895.

Bida shows the bent figure of Judas retreating into the darkness.

Hofmann, Plate 130, continues the story. "And he took a cup, and gave thanks, and gave it to them, saying, Drink ye all of it; for this is my blood of the covenant, which is shed for many unto remission of sins." (Matt. 26:27-28.)

[Illustration: The Last Supper.] Plate 130. *The Last Supper.* H. Hofmann. 1824-

No one has portrayed more clearly the characteristic attitudes of the disciples who heard these astonishing words. John is the only one who seems to appreciate the meaning of the sacrament. John only seems to have recalled distinctly what followed--the touching and comforting farewell discourses.

Hofmann, as well as Bida, shows the retreating Judas, going out into the night. "And when they had sung a hymn, they went out unto the mount of Olives." (Mark 14:26.)

"And they came unto a place which was named Gethesame; and he said unto his disciples, Sit ye here, while I go yonder and pray." (Mark 14:32, Matt. 26:36.)

Hofmann, Plate 136, reveals to us the Master in prayer, with Peter, James, and John in the distance. (Mark 14:33.) The moment is that when Jesus triumphs with the words, "Thy will be done." (Matt. 26:42.)

[Illustration: Jesus in Gethsemane.] Plate 136. *Jesus in Gethsemane.* H. Hofmann. 1824-

Dolci, Plate 135, shows the angel which came and strengthened him. (Luke 22:43.) The angel bears the cross and the cup as symbols, but the cup brought that which was sufficient to the occasion. (Compare II. Cor. 12:9.)

[Illustration: Agony in the Garden.] Plate 135. *Agony in the Garden.* Carlo Dolci. 1616-1686.

Jesus returned to the sleeping disciples. "Look," he said, "my betrayer is close at hand." He had hardly said the words when Judas came in sight with a crowd of people with swords and staffs. Judas came to Jesus and exclaimed, "I am glad to see you, Rabbi," and kissed him. (Twentieth Century N. T., Matt. 26:46-50.)

Scheffer, Plate 137, attempts to place the two characters, Jesus and Judas, in strong contrast before our eyes; but he hardly touches even the outside!

[Illustration: Kiss of Judas.] Plate 137. *Kiss of Judas.* Ary Scheffer.

Hofmann, Plate 138, represents the captive Christ. Judas, smitten already with remorse, skulks along clutching his bag of silver. Mary is watching from a distance. John is weeping upon Peter's neck. "So the band and the chief captain and the officers of the Jews, seized Jesus, and bound him, and led him to Annas." (John 18:12-13.) Simon Peter and another disciple followed Jesus afar off, and managed to gain admittance to the court of the high priest's house. There Peter denied his Lord.

[Illustration: Jesus Taken Captive.] Plate 138. *Jesus Taken Captive.* H. Hofmann. 1824-

West, Plate 140, represents Peter denying before the maid-servant (John 18:17), evidently the first time, for he was more violent the second time the maid questioned him. (Mark 14:70-71.) The painter has introduced the figure of Jesus to make the picture more intelligible. The maid seems to be asking Jesus if Peter has told the truth.

[Illustration: Peter's Denial of Christ.] Plate 140. *Peter's Denial of Christ.* Benjamin West. 1738-1820.

Harrach, Plate 139, gives the denial of Peter before the soldiers in the presence of the maid-servant. (Mark 14:54 and 67.) As Peter denies, the cock, above in the branches of a vine, crows as Jesus had predicted. Harrach has seized upon the moment recorded by Luke alone. "And the Lord turned and looked upon Peter." (Luke 22:61.) And Peter remembered, and went out and wept bitterly. (Verse 6.)

[Illustration: Peter's Denial of Christ.] Plate 139. *Peter's Denial of Christ*. Graf Harrach.

In the morning the trial is continued before Pilate. Probably no one has painted that scene so well as has *Munkacsy, Plate 141*. The picture is true to the accounts of the evangelists, and is besides a great study of character. The face of Christ is about the only inadequate piece of representation in the whole picture. Munkacsy has evidently followed Luke's account. "And they began to accuse him, saying, We found this man perverting our nation, and forbidding to give tribute to Cæsar." The moment may be that after which Pilate says, "I find no fault in this man," and the accusers "become more urgent, saying, He stirreth up the people" (Luke 23:4, 5).

[Illustration: Trial Before Pilate.] Plate 141. *Trial Before Pilate*. M'Haly Munkacsy. 1846-

Then the soldiers took Jesus into the Pretorium, and stripped him, and scourged him, and plaited a crown of thorns, and gave him a scarlet robe, and put a reed in his hand. Smiting him again and again on the head, they offered him mock reverence.

Guido, Plate 142, portrays Jesus at this time (Matt. 27:27-30). Afterwards Pilate brings Jesus forth to the crowd and says, "Behold the Man." (John 19:5.)

[Illustration: Ecce Homo.] Plate 142. *Ecce Homo*. Guido Reni. 1575-1642.

Ciseri, Plate 143, takes us upon the colonnade with Pilate and Jesus, and gives us a sense of the mad crowd below--immense, implacable--shouting "Crucify him! Crucify him!" (John 19:6.)

[Illustration: Ecce Homo.] Plate 143. *Ecce Homo*. Antonio Ciseri. 1825-

Hofmann, Plate 144, shows "the man" to us, and says, Behold him! Hofmann too, suggests the angry crowd, and in the distance introduces the three Marys. Both these artists include Pilate's wife in the picture because of Matt. 27:19.

[Illustration: Ecce Homo.] Plate 144. *Ecce Homo.* H. Hofmann. 1824-

Doré, Plate 145, with his love of the extraordinary, has objectified such a dream as he supposes might have caused a Roman matron to 'suffer many things.' She sees the living and the dead, all heaven and hell attendant upon the Christ, and because of this fears for the welfare of her husband if he does not protect so august a person as this mysterious King, whose Kingdom is not of this world.

[Illustration: Pilate's Wife's Dream.] Plate 145. *Pilate's Wife's Dream.* Gustave Doré. 1833-1883.

THE CRUCIFIXION.

Pilate at last delivered Jesus over to be crucified. "And he went out bearing the cross for himself." Through loss of sleep and loss of blood, worn out with the long agony, Jesus fainted, and fell beneath the load of the cross. They compelled a man whom they met coming in from the country, Simon the Cyrenean, to bear the cross for Jesus, and thus, accompanied by a crowd of people, they came at last to Calvary. The scene which followed has been painted hundreds of times, as a whole, and in detail, sometimes with almost revolting realism, sometimes with fascinating power.

Hofmann, Plate 146, represents Jesus carrying the cross to Calvary (John 19:17), and the women who bewailed and lamented him. (Luke 23:27.) The company is just going through the Damascus gate.

[Illustration: Bearing the Cross.] Plate 146. *Bearing the Cross.* H. Hofmann. 1824-

Thiersch, Plate 147, gives the tragic incident which occurred just outside the gate. Jesus has fallen. He is speaking to the women the words recorded in Luke 23:28-31. Calvary is seen in the distance where the crosses for the two thieves have already been placed. There they crucified him between the two thieves.

[Illustration: Bearing the Cross.] Plate 147. *Bearing the Cross.* Ludwig Thiersch.

Munkacsy, Plate 149, gives us a picture of the retreating soldiers after the awful deed has been done. "The people stood beholding . . . the rulers scoffed at him, the chief priests mocked, the scribes said, He saved others; himself he cannot save." (Luke 23:35, Mark 15:31.) Darkness is coming upon the earth. In *Plate 150,* John and the three Marys are at the foot of the cross. (John 19:25.)

[Illustration: The Crucifixion.] Plate 149. *The Crucifixion.* M. Munkacsy. 1844-

[Illustration: Christ on the Cross and the Three Marys.] Plate 150. *Christ on the Cross and the Three Marys.* M. Munkacsy. 1844-

Hofmann, Plate 148, has chosen a later moment. Jesus has committed his mother to the care of John (John 19:26-27), and with the word, "It is finished," has given up his spirit into his Father's hands. (Luke 23:46.) Amid rending rocks and opening tombs the Centurion is saying, "Truly this was the Son of God." (Matt. 27:54.)

[Illustration: The Crucifixion.] Plate 148. *The Crucifixion.* H. Hofmann. 1824-

Rubens, Plate 151, illustrates most graphically Mark 15:42-47. Joseph of Arimathæa went boldly to Pilate and asked for the body of Jesus. His request being granted, "he brought a linen cloth, and taking him down, wound him in the linen cloth." (Mark 15:46.) "And there came also Nicodemus, bringing a mixture of myrrh and aloes." So they took the body of Jesus and bound it in linen cloths, with the spices, as the custom of the Jews is to bury. (John 19:39-40.)

[Illustration: Descent from the Cross.] Plate 151. *Descent from the Cross.* Rubens. 1577-1640.

Gerome, Plate 153, has given the most weird and graphic representation of the deserted hill and the doomed city. The supernatural darkness is passing. A flood of lurid light pours upon Calvary, casting the ominous shadows of the crosses towards the retreating multitude. In the distance the livid temple marks the place of the rending veil. (Mark 15:38.)

[Illustration: Golgotha.] Plate 153. *Golgotha.* J. L. Gerome. 1824-

Morris, Plate 152, has drawn the deserted cross. An unknown woman lifts her little boy that he may see that which was written above the head of Christ. "And there was written, Jesus of Nazareth, The King of the Jews . . . in Hebrew, in Latin, and in Greek." (John 19:19-22.)

[Illustration: Whereon They Crucified Him.] Plate 152. *Whereon They Crucified Him.* P. R. Morris.

THE BURIAL.

Ciseri, Plate 156, portrays, if not "The grandest funeral that ever passed on earth," certainly the greatest. Joseph of Arimathæa, Nicodemus, and John the beloved carry the dead Christ. His mother, Mary, the Wonderful, walks by his side. "Is it nothing to you, all ye that pass by? Behold, and see if there be any sorrow like unto my sorrow, which is done unto me, wherewith the Lord hath afflicted me." (Lam. 1:12.) Mary, the wife of Clopas, Mary Magdalene, and probably Mary of Bethany, are the other mourners. "Now in the place where he was crucified there was a garden, and in the garden a new tomb wherein was never man yet laid." (John 19:41.)

[Illustration: Christ Borne to the Tomb.] Plate 156. *Christ Borne to the Tomb.* Antonio Ciseri.

Hofmann, Plate 155, represents the company entering the rock-hewn tomb. He composes his company differently. The four women are present in the background, but now two of Joseph's servants have arrived to assist the three men who had been carrying the body. There, in the tomb, the body of Jesus was laid (John 19:42).

[Illustration: Entombment.] Plate 155. *Entombment.* H. Hofmann. 1824-

Hofmann, Plate 154, adds a human touch not found in the records of the evangelists. The last to leave the body are John and the Lord's mother, Mary.

[Illustration: In the Sepulchre.] Plate 154. *In the Sepulchre.* H. Hofmann. 1824-

Dyce, Plate 158, shows John and Mary with the crown of thorns, on their way to John's own home. (John 19:27.) Joseph and Nicodemus are just leaving the garden, while Mary Magdalene and another Mary watch at the tomb. (Mark 15:47.)

[Illustration: John and the Mother of Jesus.] Plate 158. *John and the Mother of Jesus.* Wm. Dyce.

Dobson, Plate 157, has attempted to express the sorrow of Mary and the solicitude of John as they continue the walk homeward.

[Illustration: John and the Mother of Jesus.] Plate 157. *John and the Mother of Jesus.* W. C. T. Dobson.

THE RESURRECTION.

As it began to dawn towards the first day of the week, "there was a great earthquake, for an angel of the Lord descended from heaven, and came and rolled away the stone and sat upon it." (Matt. 28:1-2.)

Naack, Plate 159, has designed a panel which presents a synthesis of the various accounts of the resurrection, and adds the symbols of victory and triumph. Other artists have given more literal renderings of particular texts. For example:

[Illustration: The Resurrection.] Plate 159. *The Resurrection.* A. Naack.

Hofmann, Plate 160, has Mary sitting upon the stone outside the tomb, weeping (John 20:11), and the risen Christ approaching her from behind.

[Illustration: Easter Morning.] Plate 160. *Easter Morning.* H. Hofmann. 1824-

Di Credi, Plate 162, has selected the instant when Mary, turning, appeals to "the gardener," as she supposes, to show her where the body of Jesus has been hidden. (John 20:14-15.)

[Illustration: Christ Appearing to Magdalene.] Plate 162. *Christ Appearing to Magdalene.* Lorenzo Di Credi. 1459- 1537.

Plockhörst, Plate 161, expresses the joyful surprise of Mary when she recognizes her Lord. Jesus is directing her to go to his brethren and say, "I ascend unto my Father and your Father, and my God and your God." (John 20:17.) One hand is held as a warning to Mary not to touch him, the other points upward towards heaven.

[Illustration: Risen Lord and Mary Magdalene.] Plate 161. *Risen Lord and Mary Magdalene.* B. Plockhörst. 1825-

AFTER THE RESURRECTION.

In the afternoon, after the resurrection, two disciples on the way to Emmaus found themselves accompanied by a stranger with wondrous power as an expositor of scripture. (Luke 24:13-27.)

Plockhörst, Plate 164, takes us along the road with the three. The speaker is asking, "Was not the Christ bound to undergo all this before entering upon his glory?" (Verse 26.)

[Illustration: Walk to Emmaus.] Plate 164. *Walk to Emmaus.* B. Plockhörst. 1825-

Scheffer, Plate 163, shows Mary of Magdala, Mary the mother of James, and another woman who, after their vision at the sepulchre, are on their way to tell the disciples. (Luke 24:9-10.) These are the women whose words seemed to the disciples but idle tales unworthy of belief. (Verse 11.)

[Illustration: Three Marys.] Plate 163. *Three Marys.* Ary Scheffer. 1795-1858.

Hofmann, Plate 166, shows the two urging the stranger to stop at Emmaus. (Verses 28, 29.)

[Illustration: Walk to Emmaus.] Plate 166. *Walk to Emmaus.* H. Hofmann. 1824-

Fürst, Plate 165, shows them inviting him into the house. (Verse 29.)

[Illustration: Walk to Emmaus.] Plate 165. *Walk to Emmaus.* M. Fürst.

Müller, Plate 167, illustrates verse 30, "he took the bread and blessed it."

[Illustration: Supper at Emmaus.] Plate 167. *Supper at Emmaus.* Carl Müller. 1839-

Diethe, Plate 168, shows him in the act of breaking the bread.

[Illustration: Supper at Emmaus.] Plate 168. *Supper at Emmaus.* Alfred Diethe. 1836-

In the picture of *Rembrandt, Plate 169,* the glory appears, and the disciples recognize the Master "in the breaking of the bread." (Verses 31 and 35.)

[Illustration: Supper at Emmaus.] Plate 169. *Supper at Emmaus.* Rembrandt 1607-1669.

That very evening at Jerusalem, Jesus appeared to the disciples who were gathered in an upper room. Thomas, one of the twelve, was absent, and doubted when the others told him that they had seen the Lord. (John 20:24, 25.)

Eight days later the disciples were again together, Thomas being with them. Suddenly Jesus stood in the midst. (John 20:26.)

Guercino, Plate 170, shows what followed. "Then said he to Thomas, reach hither thy finger and see my hand, and reach hither thy hand and put it into my side; and be not faithless, but believing." (John 20:27.) The painter has given Jesus a banner as a symbol of victory, a Christian symbol as old as the catacombs.

[Illustration: "Thomas the Doubter."] Plate 170. *"Thomas the Doubter."* Guercino. 1590-1666.

THE ASCENSION.

At the end of forty days Jesus appeared to the disciples once more, and after giving final instructions as to their future work, "he led them out until they were over against Bethany: and he lifted up his hands and blessed them." (Luke 24:50.)

Hofmann, Plate 171, illustrates the next verse. "And it came to pass, while he blessed them, he parted from them, and was carried up into heaven." In Acts the added information is given that "a cloud received him out of their sight." (Acts 1:9.) Luke says, "they worshipped him" (verse 52); but Hofmann has angels worshipping (the "two men" of Acts 1:10), for the disciples are too greatly astonished to worship just then.

[Illustration: The Ascension.] Plate 171. *The Ascension.* H. Hofmann. 1824-

Rembrandt, Plate 172, emphasizes the glory of it all. The prayer of Christ (John 17:5), is answered, the promise of God (John 12:28), is fulfilled. The Spirit which appeared at the baptism of Jesus in the form of a dove, descending upon him as he began his ministry, here descends again as he enters the heavens where he ever liveth to make intercession for us.

[Illustration: The Ascension.] Plate 172. *The Ascension.* Rembrandt. 1607-1666.

And many other such pictures have been painted, which are not given in this book; but these are given that ye may be helped to see Jesus the Christ, the Son of God, and that seeing ye may believe and have life in his name.

Write the vision, and make it plain upon tables, that he may run that readeth it.

HABAKKUK 2:2.

INDEX BY TITLES OF PICTURES.

Healing the Sick Child--MAX Holy Family--MURILLO Holy
Night--CORREGGIO I am the Light of the World--HUNT Infancy of
Christ--HOFMANN In the Sepulchre--HOFMANN In the
Temple--HOFMANN Jesus and His Disciples Going through
Cornfield--DORÉ Jesus and the Child--BALLHEIM Jesus and the
Tribute Money--DORÉ Jesus and the Woman of Samaria--BILIVERTI
DORÉ HOFMANN Jesus Anoints the Blind Man's
Eyes--THEOTOCOPULI Jesus in Gethsemane--HOFMANN Jesus in
the House of Simon--VERONESE Jesus on His Way to
Jerusalem--MENGELBERG Jesus Preaches from a Boat--HOFMANN
Jesus Taken Captive--HOFMANN Jesus Walking by the
Sea--GRUNEWALD Jesus Washes the Disciples' Feet--BROWN John
and the Mother of Jesus--DOBSON DYCE John the Baptist--SARTO
John the Baptist Preaching--TITIAN Joseph and Mary; Arrival at
Bethlehem--MERSON Joseph's Dream--CRESPI Kiss of
Judas--SCHEFFER Last Supper--BIDA HOFMANN VINCI Lost Piece
of Money--MILLAIS Lost Sheep--MOLITOR Madonna and
Child--MURILLO Magdalen--RUBENS Marriage Feast--VERONESE
Mary's Visit to Elizabeth--ALBERTINELLI Miracle of the Loaves and
Fishes--MURILLO Miraculous Draught of Fishes--RAPHAEL
Nativity--BOUGUEREAU MÜLLER Nicodemus' Visit to
Jesus--UNKNOWN Parable of the Sower--ROBERT Parable of the
Virgins--POLOTY Peace, be still--DORÉ Peter's Denial of
Christ--HARRACH WEST Pharisee and Publican--DORÉ Pilate's
Wife's Dream--DORÉ Prayer in Secret--BIDA Presentation at the
Temple--BARTOLOMMEO BORGOGNONE BOURDON
CHAMPAIGNE FATTORINO Prodigal Son--DORÉ DUBUFE
MOLITOR Purification of the Temple--HOFMANN Raising of
Lazarus--BONIFAZIO PIOMBO RUBENS Raising the Daughter of
Jairus--KELLER Raising the Widow's Son--HOFMANN Repose in
Egypt--BENZ MERSON Resurrection--NAACK Rich Man and
Lazarus--DORÉ Risen Lord and Mary Magdalene--PLOCKHÖRST
Sermon on the Mount--DORÉ HOFMANN Shadow of Death--HUNT
Shadow of the Cross--MORRIS Supper at Emmaus--DIETHE MÜLLER
REMBRANDT Talking with Lame Man, Bethesda--VAN DYCK
Temptation--HOFMANN Temptation of Christ--SCHEFFER Thomas
the Doubter--GUERCINO Three Marys--SCHEFFER
Transfiguration--RAPHAEL Trial before Pilate--MUNKACSY Tribute
Money--VAN DYCK Tribute to Caesar--TITIAN Triumphal

Entry--DEGER Walk to Emmaus--FÜRST HOFMANN PLOCKHÖRST Whereon they Crucified Him--MORRIS Widow's Mite--DORÉ Worship of the Magi--HOFMANN

NOTE.--The "Wilde Bible Pictures," from which are selected the pictures illustrating "The Great Painters' Gospel," are two-and-one-half times as large as the reduction herein used. A catalogue of these penny pictures will be furnished on application to the publishers.

INDEX BY ARTISTS.

Christ Hofmann Anointing feet of Jesus Annunciation to Mary
Ascension Bearing the Cross Bethany Bethlehem Christ and the
Sinner Christ and the Young Ruler Christ Blessing Little Children
Christ Disputing with the Doctors Crucifixion Daughter of Jairus Easter
Morning Ecce Homo Entombment Flight into Egypt Healing the Sick
Infancy of Christ In the Sepulchre In the Temple Jesus and the Woman
of Samaria Jesus in Gethsemane Jesus Preaches from a Boat Jesus
taken Captive Last Supper Purification of the Temple Raising the
Widow's Son Sermon on the Mount Temptation Walk to Emmaus
Worship of the Magi Hunt, Holman. Finding of Christ in the Temple I
am the Light of the World Shadow of Death Keller, A. Raising the
Daughter of Jairus Kirchbuch, F Christ Casting out the
Money-changers Lafon, Émile, J. Christ among the Doctors Le Jeune,
Henry. Consider the Lilies Lerolle, Henry. Arrival of the Shepherds
Luini. Adoration of the Magi Maldini, Battista. Adoration of the Kings
Max, Gabriel. Healing the Sick Child Mengleberg. Jesus, Twelve Years
Old, on his Way to Jerusalem Merson, Oliver L. Joseph and Mary at
Bethlehem Repose in Egypt Millais, Sir John. Lost Piece of Money
Molitor, Franz. Lost Sheep Prodigal Son Morris, P. R. Shadow of the
Cross Whereon they Crucified Him Müller, Carl. Nativity Supper at
Emmaus Müller, Franz. Annunciation to Mary Munkacsy. Christ on the
Cross and the Three Marys Crucifixion Trial before Pilate Murillo. Holy
Family Madonna and Child Miracle of the Loaves and Fishes Naack,
A. Resurrection Overbeck. Behold, I Stand at the Door and Knock
Piombo, Sebastian del. Raising of Lazarus Plockhörst. Angels and the
Shepherds Christ and St. Peter Christ Blessing Little Children Christ
Taking Leave of His Mother Christ the Consoler Flight into Egypt Good
Shepherd Risen Lord and Mary Magdalene Walk to Emmaus Poloty,
Theodore von Parable of the Virgins Pordenone, Giovanni. Calling of
Matthew Raphael. Christ's Charge to St. Peter Demoniac Boy
Miraculous Draught of Fishes Transfiguration Rembrandt. Ascension
Supper at Emmaus Reni, Guido. Annunciation to Mary Christ Giving
Keys to St. Peter Ecce Homo Head of John the Baptist in a Charger
Richter, Gustav. Christ Raising the Daughter of Jairus Robert, H. L.
Parable of the Sower Rubens. Descent from the Cross Magdalen
Raising of Lazarus Sarto, Andrea del. John the Baptist Scheffer, Ary.
Kiss of Judas Temptation of Christ Three Marys Schönherr, Karl. Good
Shepherd Healing the Sick Schwartz. Christ and St. Peter Siemenroth,
K. Good Samaritan Signol, Emile. Adulterous Woman Theotocopuli.

Jesus Anoints the Blind Man's Eyes Thiersch, Ludwig. Bearing the Cross Titian. Annunciation John the Baptist Preaching Tribute to Caesar Unknown Artist. Nicodemus' Visit to Jesus Van Dyck. Talking with Lame Man, Bethesda Tribute Money Van Lint, Peter. Healing of the Impotent Man Vecchio, Palma. Canaanitish Woman Veronese, Bonifazio. Adoration of the Magi Veronese, Paolo. Centurion's Servant Marriage Feast Jesus in the House of Simon Vinci, Leonardo Da. Last Supper Vogel, Carlo. Christ Blessing Little Children West, Benjamin. Peter's Denial of Christ Zimmermann, Ernst K.G. Christ and the Fishermen

---

End of Project Gutenberg's The Great Painters' Gospel, by Henry Turner Bailey

do practically ANYTHING with public domain eBooks. Redistribution is subject to the trademark license, especially commercial redistribution.

*** START: FULL LICENSE ***

THE FULL PROJECT GUTENBERG LICENSE PLEASE READ THIS BEFORE YOU DISTRIBUTE OR USE THIS WORK

To protect the Project Gutenberg-tm mission of promoting the free distribution of electronic works, by using or distributing this work (or any other work associated in any way with the phrase "Project Gutenberg"), you agree to comply with all the terms of the Full Project Gutenberg-tm License (available with this file or online at http://gutenberg.net/license).

Section 1. General Terms of Use and Redistributing Project Gutenberg-tm electronic works

1.A. By reading or using any part of this Project Gutenberg-tm electronic work, you indicate that you have read, understand, agree to and accept all the terms of this license and intellectual property (trademark/copyright) agreement. If you do not agree to abide by all the terms of this agreement, you must cease using and return or destroy all copies of Project Gutenberg-tm electronic works in your possession. If you paid a fee for obtaining a copy of or access to a Project Gutenberg-tm electronic work and you do not agree to be bound by the terms of this agreement, you may obtain a refund from the person or entity to whom you paid the fee as set forth in paragraph 1.E.8.

1.B. "Project Gutenberg" is a registered trademark. It may only be used on or associated in any way with an electronic work by people who agree to be bound by the terms of this agreement. There are a few things that you can do with most Project Gutenberg-tm electronic works even without complying with the full terms of this agreement. See paragraph 1.C below. There are a lot of things you can do with Project Gutenberg-tm electronic works if you follow the terms of this agreement and help preserve free future access to Project Gutenberg-tm electronic works. See paragraph 1.E below.

with this eBook or online at www.gutenberg.net

1.E.2. If an individual Project Gutenberg-tm electronic work is derived from the public domain (does not contain a notice indicating that it is posted with permission of the copyright holder), the work can be copied and distributed to anyone in the United States without paying any fees or charges. If you are redistributing or providing access to a work with the phrase "Project Gutenberg" associated with or appearing on the work, you must comply either with the requirements of paragraphs 1.E.1 through 1.E.7 or obtain permission for the use of the work and the Project Gutenberg-tm trademark as set forth in paragraphs 1.E.8 or 1.E.9.

1.E.3. If an individual Project Gutenberg-tm electronic work is posted with the permission of the copyright holder, your use and distribution must comply with both paragraphs 1.E.1 through 1.E.7 and any additional terms imposed by the copyright holder. Additional terms will be linked to the Project Gutenberg-tm License for all works posted with the permission of the copyright holder found at the beginning of this work.

1.E.4. Do not unlink or detach or remove the full Project Gutenberg-tm License terms from this work, or any files containing a part of this work or any other work associated with Project Gutenberg-tm.

1.E.5. Do not copy, display, perform, distribute or redistribute this electronic work, or any part of this electronic work, without prominently displaying the sentence set forth in paragraph 1.E.1 with active links or immediate access to the full terms of the Project Gutenberg-tm License.

1.E.6. You may convert to and distribute this work in any binary, compressed, marked up, nonproprietary or proprietary form, including any word processing or hypertext form. However, if you provide access to or distribute copies of a Project Gutenberg-tm work in a format other than "Plain Vanilla ASCII" or other format used in the official version posted on the official Project Gutenberg-tm web site (www.gutenberg.net), you must, at no additional cost, fee or expense to the user, provide a copy, a means of exporting a copy, or a means of obtaining a copy upon request, of the work in its original "Plain Vanilla ASCII" or other form. Any alternate format must include the full Project Gutenberg-tm License as specified in paragraph 1.E.1.

1.E.7. Do not charge a fee for access to, viewing, displaying, performing, copying or distributing any Project Gutenberg-tm works unless you comply with paragraph 1.E.8 or 1.E.9.

1.E.8. You may charge a reasonable fee for copies of or providing access to or distributing Project Gutenberg-tm electronic works provided that

- You pay a royalty fee of 20% of the gross profits you derive from the use of Project Gutenberg-tm works calculated using the method you already use to calculate your applicable taxes. The fee is owed to the owner of the Project Gutenberg-tm trademark, but he has agreed to donate royalties under this paragraph to the Project Gutenberg Literary Archive Foundation. Royalty payments must be paid within 60 days following each date on which you prepare (or are legally required to prepare) your periodic tax returns. Royalty payments should be clearly marked as such and sent to the Project Gutenberg Literary Archive Foundation at the address specified in Section 4, "Information about donations to the Project Gutenberg Literary Archive Foundation."

- You provide a full refund of any money paid by a user who notifies you in writing (or by e-mail) within 30 days of receipt that s/he does not agree to the terms of the full Project Gutenberg-tm License. You must require such a user to return or destroy all copies of the works possessed in a physical medium and discontinue all use of and all access to other copies of Project Gutenberg-tm works.

- You provide, in accordance with paragraph 1.F.3, a full refund of any money paid for a work or a replacement copy, if a defect in the electronic work is discovered and reported to you within 90 days of receipt of the work.

- You comply with all other terms of this agreement for free distribution of Project Gutenberg-tm works.

1.E.9. If you wish to charge a fee or distribute a Project Gutenberg-tm electronic work or group of works on different terms than are set forth in this agreement, you must obtain permission in writing from both the Project Gutenberg Literary Archive Foundation and Michael Hart, the owner of the Project Gutenberg-tm trademark. Contact the Foundation as set forth in Section 3 below.

1.F.

1.F.1. Project Gutenberg volunteers and employees expend considerable effort to identify, do copyright research on, transcribe and proofread public domain works in creating the Project Gutenberg-tm collection. Despite these efforts, Project Gutenberg-tm electronic works, and the medium on which they may be stored, may contain "Defects," such as, but not limited to, incomplete, inaccurate or corrupt data, transcription errors, a copyright or other intellectual property infringement, a defective or damaged disk or other medium, a computer virus, or computer codes that damage or cannot be read by your equipment.

1.F.2. LIMITED WARRANTY, DISCLAIMER OF DAMAGES - Except for the "Right of Replacement or Refund" described in paragraph 1.F.3, the Project Gutenberg Literary Archive Foundation, the owner of the Project Gutenberg-tm trademark, and any other party distributing a Project Gutenberg-tm electronic work under this agreement, disclaim all liability to you for damages, costs and expenses, including legal fees. YOU AGREE THAT YOU HAVE NO REMEDIES FOR NEGLIGENCE, STRICT LIABILITY, BREACH OF WARRANTY OR BREACH OF CONTRACT EXCEPT THOSE PROVIDED IN PARAGRAPH 1.F.3. YOU AGREE THAT THE FOUNDATION, THE TRADEMARK OWNER, AND ANY DISTRIBUTOR UNDER THIS AGREEMENT WILL NOT BE LIABLE TO YOU FOR ACTUAL, DIRECT, INDIRECT, CONSEQUENTIAL, PUNITIVE OR INCIDENTAL DAMAGES EVEN IF YOU GIVE NOTICE OF THE POSSIBILITY OF SUCH DAMAGE.

1.F.3. LIMITED RIGHT OF REPLACEMENT OR REFUND - If you discover a defect in this electronic work within 90 days of receiving it, you can receive a refund of the money (if any) you paid for it by sending a written explanation to the person you received the work from. If you received the work on a physical medium, you must return the medium with your written explanation. The person or entity that provided you with the defective work may elect to provide a replacement copy in lieu of a refund. If you received the work electronically, the person or entity providing it to you may choose to give you a second opportunity to receive the work electronically in lieu of a refund. If the second copy is also defective, you may demand a refund in writing without further opportunities to fix the problem.

1.F.4. Except for the limited right of replacement or refund set forth in paragraph 1.F.3, this work is provided to you 'AS-IS' WITH NO OTHER WARRANTIES OF ANY KIND, EXPRESS OR IMPLIED, INCLUDING BUT NOT LIMITED TO WARRANTIES OF MERCHANTIBILITY OR FITNESS FOR ANY PURPOSE.

1.F.5. Some states do not allow disclaimers of certain implied warranties or the exclusion or limitation of certain types of damages. If any disclaimer or limitation set forth in this agreement violates the law of the state applicable to this agreement, the agreement shall be interpreted to make the maximum disclaimer or limitation permitted by the applicable state law. The invalidity or unenforceability of any provision of this agreement shall not void the remaining provisions.

1.F.6. **INDEMNITY**

- You agree to indemnify and hold the Foundation, the trademark owner, any agent or employee of the Foundation, anyone providing copies of Project Gutenberg-tm electronic works in accordance with this agreement, and any volunteers associated with the production, promotion and distribution of Project Gutenberg-tm electronic works, harmless from all liability, costs and expenses, including legal fees, that arise directly or indirectly from any of the following which you do or cause to occur: (a) distribution of this or any Project Gutenberg-tm work, (b) alteration, modification, or additions or deletions to any Project Gutenberg-tm work, and (c) any Defect you cause.

Section 2. Information about the Mission of Project Gutenberg-tm

Project Gutenberg-tm is synonymous with the free distribution of electronic works in formats readable by the widest variety of computers including obsolete, old, middle-aged and new computers. It exists because of the efforts of hundreds of volunteers and donations from people in all walks of life.

Volunteers and financial support to provide volunteers with the assistance they need are critical to reaching Project Gutenberg-tm's goals and ensuring that the Project Gutenberg-tm collection will remain freely available for generations to come. In 2001, the Project Gutenberg Literary Archive Foundation was created to provide a secure and permanent future for Project Gutenberg-tm and future generations. To learn more about the Project Gutenberg Literary Archive Foundation and how your efforts and donations can help, see Sections 3 and 4 and the Foundation web page at http://www.pglaf.org.

Section 3. Information about the Project Gutenberg Literary Archive Foundation

The Project Gutenberg Literary Archive Foundation is a non profit 501(c)(3) educational corporation organized under the laws of the state of Mississippi and granted tax exempt status by the Internal Revenue Service. The Foundation's EIN or federal tax identification number is 64-6221541. Its 501(c)(3) letter is posted at http://pglaf.org/fundraising. Contributions to the Project Gutenberg Literary Archive Foundation are tax deductible to the full extent permitted by U.S. federal laws and your state's laws.

The Foundation's principal office is located at 4557 Melan Dr. S. Fairbanks, AK, 99712., but its volunteers and employees are scattered throughout numerous locations. Its business office is located at 809 North 1500 West, Salt Lake City, UT 84116, (801) 596-1887, email business@pglaf.org. Email contact links and up to date contact information can be found at the Foundation's web site and official page at http://pglaf.org

For additional contact information: Dr. Gregory B. Newby Chief Executive and Director gbnewby@pglaf.org

Section 4. Information about Donations to the Project Gutenberg Literary Archive Foundation

Project Gutenberg-tm depends upon and cannot survive without wide spread public support and donations to carry out its mission of increasing the number of public domain and licensed works that can be freely distributed in machine readable form accessible by the widest array of equipment including outdated equipment. Many small donations ($1 to $5,000) are particularly important to maintaining tax exempt status with the IRS.

The Foundation is committed to complying with the laws regulating charities and charitable donations in all 50 states of the United States. Compliance requirements are not uniform and it takes a considerable effort, much paperwork and many fees to meet and keep up with these requirements. We do not solicit donations in locations where we have not received written confirmation of compliance. To SEND DONATIONS or determine the status of compliance for any particular state visit http://pglaf.org

While we cannot and do not solicit contributions from states where we have not met the solicitation requirements, we know of no prohibition against accepting unsolicited donations from donors in such states who approach us with offers to donate.

International donations are gratefully accepted, but we cannot make any statements concerning tax treatment of donations received from outside the United States. U.S. laws alone swamp our small staff.

Please check the Project Gutenberg Web pages for current donation methods and addresses. Donations are accepted in a number of other ways including including checks, online payments and credit card donations. To donate, please visit: http://pglaf.org/donate

Section 5. General Information About Project Gutenberg-tm electronic works.

Professor Michael S. Hart is the originator of the Project Gutenberg-tm concept of a library of electronic works that could be freely shared with

---

Great Painters' Gospel, by Henry Turner Bailey